A Listening/ Speaking Skills Book

mosaic one

A Listening/ Speaking Skills Book

With Learning Strategies and Language Functions

Jami Ferrer-Hanreddy
Trainer/Consultant
Milwaukee, Wisconsin

Elizabeth Whalley
San Francisco State University

The McGraw-Hill Companies, Inc.

New York   St. Louis   San Francisco   Auckland   Bogotá   Caracas   Lisbon
London   Madrid   Mexico City   Milan   Montreal   New Delhi   San Juan
Singapore   Sydney   Tokyo   Toronto

This is an  book.

McGraw-Hill

A Division of The McGraw-Hill Companies

Mosaic One
A Listening/Speaking Skills Book
Third Edition

1 2 3 4 5 6 7 8 9 0   DOC   DOC   9 0 9 8 7 6

ISBN 0-07-020634-1
ISBN 0-07-114510-9

This book was set in Times Roman by Monotype Composition Company, Inc.

The editors were Tim Stookesberry, Bill Preston, and John Chapman; the designers were Lorna
Lo, Suzanne Montazer, Francis Owens, and Elizabeth Williamson; the production supervisor
was Phyllis Snyder; the project editor was Stacey Sawyer; the cover was designed by Francis
Owens; the cover illustrator was Susan Pizzo; the photo researcher was Cindy Robinson,
Seaside Publishing; illustrations were done by David Bohn, Axelle Fortier, Rick Hackney,
Lori Heckelman, and Sally Richardson.

R. R. Donnelley & Sons Company, Crawfordsville, IN, was printer and binder.
Phoenix Color Corporation was cover separator and printer.

Library of Congress Catalog Card Number: 95-80834.

Photo credits: *Page 1* ©Mary Kate Denny/PhotoEdit; *3* ©Joseph Uouacs/Stock, Boston; *4*
©Jerry Berndt/Stock, Boston; *5* ©Ulrike Welsch/Photo Researchers, Inc.; *7* ©David Grossman,
Photo Researchers, Inc.; *8* ©Tom McCarthy/PhotoEdit; *9* ©Johnathan Nourok/PhotoEdit; *10*
©Fredrik D. Bodin/Stock, Boston; *14* ©David Bohn; *17* ©Joseph Schuyler/Stock, Boston; *18*
©Elizabeth Crews/Stock, Boston; *21* ©David Grossman/Photo Researchers, Inc.; *23* ©Mary
Kate Denny/PhotoEdit; *25* ©Bonnie Kamin/PhotoEdit; *26* ©Barbara Rios/Photo Researchers,
Inc.; *28* ©John Fung; *29* ©Peter Menzel/Stock, Boston; *30* ©Ray Ellis/Photo Researchers, Inc.;
31 ©Roberta Hershenson/Photo Researchers, Inc.; *32* ©Erika Stone/Photo Researchers, Inc.; *35*

(continued on page 206)

Contents

Preface to the Third Edition   xi

Summary of Listening/Speaking Exercises and Activities for Learning Strategies and Language Functions   xviii

CHAPTER **one**

New Challenges   *1*

LECTURE   "Learning to Speak Someone Else's Language"

DID YOU KNOW?   2

Sharing Your Experience   2
Vocabulary   4

SKILL A   Learning Strategy: Listening to Make Predictions   4
Listen In   5
Speak Out   7

SKILL B   Language Function: Offering and Requesting Clarification   11
Conversations   12
Listen In   13
Speak Out   14

focus on testing   16

CHAPTER **two**

Looking at Learning   *17*

LECTURE   "Learning to Listen/Listening to Learn"

DID YOU KNOW?   18

Sharing Your Experience   18
Vocabulary   20

SKILL A   Learning Strategy: Listening for the Main Ideas   21
Listen In   22
Speak Out   23

SKILL B   Language Function: Asking for Confirmation   24
Conversations   25
Listen In   26
Speak Out   27

focus on testing   28

CHAPTER **three**

Relationships

SEMINAR   "Family Networks and the Elderly"   29

DID YOU KNOW?   30

Sharing Your Experience   30
Vocabulary   31

SKILL A   Learning Strategy: Listening for Key Terms   32
Listen In   32
Speak Out   33

SKILL B   Language Function: Making Generalizations   35
Listen In   36
Speak Out   37

SKILL C   Learning Strategy: Listening for "Straw Man" Arguments   38
Listen In   38
Speak Out   39

SKILL D   Language Function: Introducing Information   40
Conversations   40
Listen In   41
Speak Out   41

focus on testing   42

CHAPTER **four**

Health

STUDY SESSION   "What Makes Us Tick: The Cardiac Muscle"   43

DID YOU KNOW?   44

Sharing Your Experience   44
Vocabulary   45

SKILL A   Learning Strategy: Listening for Analogies   45
Listen In   46
Speak Out   46

SKILL B   Language Function: Expressing Opinions   48
Conversations   48
Listen In   49
Speak Out   50

focus on testing   52

CHAPTER **five**

High Tech, Low Tech   **53**

FIELD TRIP DEMONSTRATION   "Space Flight: A Simulation"

DID YOU KNOW?   54

Sharing Your Experience   54
Vocabulary   55

SKILL A   Learning Strategy: Taking Notes on a Field Trip   56
Listen In   57
Speak Out   60

SKILL B   Language Function: Shifting Focus   60
Conversations   61
Listen In   62
Speak Out   62

focus on testing   64

CHAPTER **six**

Money Matters   **65**

RADIO PROGRAM   "The World Bank Under Fire"

DID YOU KNOW?   66

Sharing Your Experience   66
Vocabulary   67

SKILL A   Learning Strategy: Listening for Pros and Cons   68
Listen In   68
Speak Out   70

SKILL B   Language Function: Agreeing and Disagreeing   71
Conversations   72
Listen In   74
Speak Out   75

focus on testing   75

CHAPTER seven
Leisure Time 77

PUBLIC LECTURE "Leisure Time in Our Society"

DID YOU KNOW? 78

Sharing Your Experience 78
Vocabulary 80

SKILL A Learning Strategy: Listening for Chronological Order 80
Listen In 81
Speak Out 83

SKILL B Language Function: Expressing Likes and Dislikes 84
Conversations 84
Listen In 85
Speak Out 86

focus on testing 88

CHAPTER eight
Creativity 89

LECTURE "Creativity: As Essential to the Engineer as to the Artist"

DID YOU KNOW? 90

Sharing Your Experience 90
Vocabulary 92

SKILL A Learning Strategy: Listening for Signal Words 92
Listen In 93
Speak Out 94

SKILL B Language Function: Divulging Information 96
Conversations 96
Listen In 97
Speak Out 98

focus on testing 100

CHAPTER **nine**

Human Behavior   101

LECTURE   "Group Dynamics"

DID YOU KNOW?   102

Sharing Your Experience   102
Vocabulary   104

SKILL A   Learning Strategy: Recognizing Digressions   105
Listen In   106
Speak Out   109

SKILL B   Language Function: Asking for Information, Seeking Confirmation, and
                              Challenging with Tag Questions   110
Conversations   112
Listen In   113
Speak Out   114

focus on testing   116

CHAPTER **ten**

Crime and Punishment   117

LECTURE   "Choice: The Uniquely Human Problem"

DID YOU KNOW?   118

Sharing Your Experience   118
Vocabulary   120

SKILL A   Learning Strategy: Paraphrasing   121
Listen In   121
Speak Out   123

SKILL B   Language Function: Expressing Wishes, Hopes, and Desires   125
Conversations   125
Listen In   125
Speak Out   126

focus on testing   127

Contents

CHAPTER eleven

The Physical World

129

LECTURE   "Penguins at the Pole"

DID YOU KNOW?   130

Sharing Your Experience   130
Vocabulary   131

SKILL A   Learning Strategy: Outlining   132
Listen In   132
Speak Out   134

SKILL B   Language Function: Stating Reasons   134
Conversations   135
Listen In   135
Speak Out   136

focus on testing   136

CHAPTER twelve

Together on a Small Planet

137

LECTURE   "Folk Wisdom"

DID YOU KNOW?   138

Sharing Your Experience   138
Vocabulary   139

SKILL A   Learning Strategy: Summarizing   140
Listen In   141
Speak Out   143

SKILL B   Language Function: Telling a Joke   144
Conversations   145
Listen In   146
Speak Out   147

focus on testing   148

Tapescript   151

Preface
to the Third Edition

The Mosaic One Program

The Mosaic One program consists of four texts and a variety of supplemental materials for intermediate to high-intermediate students seeking to improve their English language skills. Each of the four texts in this program is carefully organized by chapter theme, vocabulary, grammar structures, and where possible, learning strategies and language functions. As a result, information introduced in a chapter of any one of the Mosaic One texts corresponds to and reinforces material taught in the same chapter of the other three books, creating a truly inte-grated, four-skills approach.

The Mosaic One program is highly flexible. The texts in this series may be used together or separately, depending on students' needs and course goals. The books in this program include:

- **A Content-Based Grammar.** Designed to teach grammar through content, this book introduces, practices, and applies grammatical structures through the development of high-interest chapter topics. This thematic approach gives students motivation because they are improving their mastery of grammatical structures and vocabulary while expanding their own knowledge.

- **A Content-Based Writing Book**. This book takes students step-by-step through the writing process—from formulating ideas through the revision stage. Writing assignments progress from paragraphs to essays, and students write about interesting, contemporary subjects from the sciences, social sciences, and humanities that are relevant to their current or future academic coursework.

- **A Listening / Speaking Skills Book.** This text teaches learning strategies and language functions, while maintaining a strong focus on both listening and speaking. Each chapter includes a realistic listening passage on an interesting topic related to the chapter theme. Short conversations also provide comprehension practice, while a variety of speaking activities reinforce the use of language in context.

- **A Reading Skills Book.** The selections in this text help students develop their reading skills in a meaningful rather than a mechanical way— enabling them to successfully tackle other academic texts. The three readings per chapter come from a variety of authentic sources, such as textbooks, magazines, newspapers, interviews, and so on, and are accompanied by pre- and post-reading exercises, including skimming, scanning, making inferences, paraphrasing, and group problem solving.

Supplemental Materials

In addition to the four core texts outlined above, various supplemental materials are available to assist users of the third edition, including:

Instructor's Manual

Extensively revised for the new edition, this manual provides instructions and guidelines for using the four core texts separately or in various combinations to suit particular program needs. For each of the core texts, there is a separate section with answer keys, teaching tips, additional activities, and other suggestions. The testing materials have been greatly expanded in this edition.

Audio Program for *Mosaic One: A Listening/Speaking Skills Book*

 Completely re-recorded for the new edition, the audio program is designed to be used in conjunction with those exercises that are indicated with a cassette icon in the student text. Complete tapescripts are now included in the back of the student text.

Audio Program to Accompany *Mosaic One: A Reading Skills Book*

 This new optional audio program contains selected readings from the student text. These taped selections of poems, articles, stories, and speeches enable students to listen at their leisure to the natural oral discourse of native readers for intonation and modeling. Readings that are included in this program are indicated with a cassette icon in the student text.

Video/Video Guide

New to this edition, the video program for Mosaic One contains authentic television segments that are coordinated with the twelve chapter themes in the four texts. A variety of pre- and postviewing exercises and activities for this video are available in a separate Video Guide.

Mosaic One: A Listening/Speaking Skills Book, Third Edition

Rationale and Chapter Organization

Mosaic One: A Listening/Speaking Skills Book, Third Edition, is unique among listening/speak-

ing materials currently available. Most other materials focus on either listening or speaking and teach either learning strategies or language functions. This text teaches learning strategies *and* language functions, while maintaining a strong focus on *both* listening and speaking.

The text consists of twelve chapters. One learning strategy and one language function are presented in each chapter (Chapter Three has two of each). Every chapter includes a realistic listening passage on a high-interest topic related to the chapter theme and is accompanied by interactive listening exercises. Short conversations also provide highly realistic listening comprehension practice. A variety of speaking activities then reinforce the use of learning strategies and language functions in context. The three main parts of each chapter can be summarized as follows:

- **Getting Started.** A section called **Sharing Your Experience** presents discussion questions designed to tap students' prior knowledge of aspects of the chapter theme. These questions are followed by a **Vocabulary** section consisting of one or more exercises that provide comprehension practice for key words that will appear in the listening passage.

- **Skill A.** This part is always a presentation of a learning strategy essential for academic success. Explanations are both thorough and easy to follow. This presentation is followed by **Listen In** exercises based on a high-interest listening passage and **Speak Out** activities designed to provide practice of the strategy in realistic contexts.

- **Skill B.** This part is always a presentation of a language function. Here, thorough and clear explanations are complemented by an abundance of useful idiomatic expressions. This presentation is followed by a **Conversations** section and **Listen In** exercises designed to promote comprehension of the language function, as well as **Speak Out** activities to provide practice of the language function and idioms in realistic contexts.

New to the Third Edition

1. **Streamlined Design.** The two-color design and revised art program make this edition more appealing to today's students. It is also more user friendly because many directions have been shortened and clarified, exercises and activities have been numbered, and key information has been highlighted in shaded boxes and charts.

2. **New Chapter Theme on Crime and Punishment.** The new edition features an entirely new theme for Chapter Ten: Crime and Punishment. In addition, themes for several other chapters have been broadened to include new content.

3. **Did You Know?** This entirely new boxed feature opens the chapter with interest-catching information designed to arouse curiosity about the chapter theme, stimulate thought and conversation, and enhance motivation for learning.

4. **Focus on Testing.** Also appearing in each chapter, this new boxed feature simulates a standardized listening test, such as the listening portion of the TOEFL. It gives students the opportunity to practice listening for information in a controlled situation, where they are not able to interact with the speaker(s) or allowed to rewind the tape and listen again.

5. **Listening Passages.** Along with the usual variety of academic lectures, listening passages are presented in a variety of other formats, including a seminar, a study session, a field trip, a radio program, and a public lecture. In addition, all listening passages have been rewritten to include interactive dialogue involving several speakers. This interactivity makes the passages more natural; at the same time, it helps break up some longer passages into more manageable "chunks" of listening material. Finally, portions of some listening passages have been edited to help make the transition in level of difficulty from *Interactions Two: A Listening/Speaking Skills Book,* Third Edition, smoother and easier.

6. **Conversations.** Conversatinons in this section, which were used in the previous edition only to illustrate language functions, are now presented with accompanying listening exercises designed to teach the use of language functions in realistic contexts.

7. **Skills Chart.** A chart summarizing the listening exercises and speaking activities follows the preface.

8. **Tapescripts.** All tapescripts are now in back of the student text.

9. **Answer Keys.** Answer keys for all exercises are in the Instructor's Manual.

General Teaching Suggestions

1. Read through an entire chapter and listen to the taped material for that chapter before teaching any portion of it.

2. The interactive comprehension and production activities are carefully designed for maximum appeal to students. Since no two classes are alike, however, activities can be readily adapted and personalized, allowing for a great deal of flexibility. For example, activities can be modified to reflect such variables as local information, current events, names of students, and students' personal interests and experiences.

3. To facilitate the various role-plays and other interactive activities, you will probably need to disinhibit yourself and the students to some degree. To this end, you can use the personal information you know about the students: What amuses them? What saddens them? What excites them? Using a few bits of personal information in a relaxed and safe environment can greatly increase both individual participation and class rapport.

4. To facilitate maximum student participation during speaking activities, allow students to

interact without interruption as much as possible unless there are misunderstandings or miscommunications. Keep notes and give feedback after students have completed an activity. In this way, you can avoid having students look to you for judgment after each sentence they utter.

5. During small group activities, heterogeneous groups—where all proficiency levels are represented—are generally recommended. However, there are occasions when it is advisable to put all of the more proficient students in one group so that they cannot dominate the less proficient students. Whether *you* place students in groups or they form their own groups, be sure to change the groupings periodically. Doing this will help promote strong class rapport as well as expose students to a greater variety of voices and speaking styles for listening practice.

6. The exercises are designed to teach skills, not to test proficiency. However, students will generally need to be reminded that it is all right to make errors. They are not expected to be competent at each task already, but rather, through the process of learning from errors, to *become* competent.

7. This text provides more practice exercises and activities in each chapter than most teachers would be able to use in a week of class time. Therefore, if you wish to complete a chapter a week, you may have to choose among the activities provided.

Specific Teaching Suggestions

Did You Know? To use this feature as a listening exercise, read each item as a question (Did you know . . . ?) and have students answer "yes" or "no." Or have students work in pairs, taking turns asking each other the questions (in this case, the student listening should close his or her book).

To use this feature as a speaking activity, discuss each item in pairs, small groups, or as a class. Students can add their own "Did You Know…?" items to the ones given in the text. As an extension activity providing reading and research practice, students can look up additional items appropriate to the chapter theme.

Sharing Your Experience. This section allows students to relate their own knowledge, background, and experience to the chapter theme. Most questions are open ended; there are no right or wrong answers, and students should be encouraged to share whatever they can. A suggested time frame for discussing these questions is about fifteen minutes. If some students are reluctant to participate at first, try having them write out their answers for homework the night before.

Vocabulary. The vocabulary exercises can be done in class or as homework. Doing them cooperatively in pairs or groups is an excellent way for students to learn the words while gaining extra speaking practice.

Skill A—Learning Strategy. Explanatory material is provided for each skill. Students can read this material at home or in class before or after you discuss the skill with them. Or you can read the material aloud to them while you put key points on the board.

Skill A—Listen In. Students listen to the passage on the cassette and do the accompanying exercises. You may need to do several items as examples and perhaps stop the tape more frequently than is suggested in the text for some groups of students.

Skill A—Speak Out. The focus here is on speaking, but the activities also involve active listening. Both whole class and small group activities are provided; these vary in length from about ten minutes to a whole class period.

Skill B—Language Function and Conversations. A language function is presented and then illustrated in a listening exercise using short conversations. This section helps students master idioms, stress and intonation patterns, and body language associated with the language function. The listening exercise is designed to teach, not test. For students who have difficulty, you may have them:

a. read along as they listen.
b. listen and repeat short selections of the conversation.
c. listen and pantomime facial expressions and gestures they think the speakers would use.
d. fill in cloze passages you have created from the conversations.

Skill B—Listen In. This section gives students the opportunity to listen for uses (or misuses) of the language function in the passage or the conversations. You may need to stop the tape frequently for some students, but you should work toward building their comprehension of increasingly longer chunks of language.

Skill B—Speak Out. These activities provide natural language contexts in which to practice the language function. They are designed to maximize student interaction and verbal output. Accordingly, you will want to provide feedback that facilitates rather than inhibits this interaction as students play the various games, participate in role-plays, or team up for debates (see item 4, under General Teaching Suggestions). The time frame for these activities can vary from ten minutes to a whole class period.

Focus on Testing. In this feature, which simulates a standardized listening test, students listen for specific information. They listen to a passage once only, then answer questions that follow. After they finish this mini-test, you should let them listen to the items again, then go over the answers and any questions they might have.

Dedication

To the memory of Cindy Strauss, Gertrude and Stanley Whalley, and Fred Goldstein.

And for Joe and Gracie, who have never read a word, yet consummately provide the context for the work in wordless ways.

Acknowledgments

First, we wish to acknowledge the expertise, imagination, and inspiration of those whose contributions to the first and second editions helped lay the foundation for the third: Marilyn Bernstein, Steven Carlson, Jill Wagner-Schimpff, Steven Hollander, and Steven Marx. We are indebted to Eirik Børve, who included us in the ground-breaking first edition project, and ever grateful to Mary McVey Gill for her monumental efforts in pulling such a project together, her most excellent editorial work, and her friendship.

We wish to express our deepest appreciation to Thalia Dorwick and Tim Stookesberry for their acumen and persistence in choosing to pursue a third edition and for treating us in style; to Bill Preston for his most excellent and unflagging editorial support; to John Chapman for his superb editorial assistance at a crucial point in the process; and to Lila M. Gardner for her ability to provide both a calming effect and desperately needed editorial wizardry when the going got tough.

Judy Tanka deserves the prize for most exceptional editor. She read every word, always had positive suggestions for problem areas, and even caught typos from the second edition!

We are also grateful to others who have provided creative suggestions and other support. Steve Aron; Connie Bendel; Mary, Louise, Elizabeth and Roger Dunn; Sue Garfield; Osha Hanfling; David Marimont; DeeDee Quinn; Ann Stromberg; Pat Sutton; and, of course, the folks down at the Plant.

We heartily acknowledge the assistance of the staff at the Palo Alto Public Library and the support of San Francisco State University.

Finally, our thanks to the following reviewers whose comments, both favorable and critical, were of great value in the development of the third edition of the Interactions/Mosaic series:

Jean Al-Sibai, University of North Carolina; Janet Alexander, Waterbury College; Roberta Alexander, San Diego City College; Julie Alpert, Santa Barbara City College; Anita Cook, Tidewater Community College; Anne Deal Beavers, Heald Business College; Larry Berking, Monroe Community College; Deborah Busch, Delaware County Community College; Patricia A. Card, Chaminade University of Honolulu; José A. Carmona, Hudson County Community College; Kathleen Carroll, Fontbonne College; Consuela Chase, Loyola University; Lee Chen, California State University; Karen Cheng, University of Malaya; Gaye Childress, University of North Texas; Maria Conforti, University of Colorado; Earsie A. de Feliz, Arkansas State University; Elizabeth Devlin-Foltz, Montgomery County Adult Education; Colleen Dick, San Francisco Institute of English; Marta Dmytrenko-Ahrabian, Wayne State University; Margo Duffy, Northeast Wisconsin Technical; Magali Duignan, Augusta College; Janet Dyar, Meridian Community College; Anne Ediger, San Diego City College; D. Frangie, Wayne State University; Robert Geryk, Wayne State University; Jeanne Gibson, American Language Academy; Kathleen Walsh Greene, Rhode Island College; Myra Harada, San Diego Mesa College; Kristin Hathhorn, Eastern Washington University; Mary Herbert, University of California, Davis; Joyce Homick, Houston Community College; Catherine Hutcheson, Texas Christian University; Suzie Johnston, Tyler Junior College; Donna Kauffman, Radford University; Emmie Lim, Cypress College; Patricia Mascarenas, Monte Vista Community School; Mark Mattison, Donnelly College; Diane Peak, Choate Rosemary Hall; James Pedersen, Irvine Valley College; Linda Quillan, Arkansas State University; Marnie Ramker, University of Illinois; Joan Roberts, The Doane Stuart School; Doralee Robertson, Jacksonville University; Ellen Rosen, Fullerton College; Jean Sawyer, American Language Academy; Frances Schulze, College of San Mateo; Sherrie R. Sellers, Brigham Young University; Tess M. Shafer, Edmonds Community College; Heinz F. Tengler, Lado International College; Sara Tipton, Wayne State University; Karen R. Vallejo, Brigham Young University; Susan Williams, University of Central Florida; Mary Shepard Wong, El Camino College; Cindy Yoder, Eastern Mennonite College; Cheryl L. Youtsey, Loyola University; Miriam Zahler, Wayne State University; Maria Zien, English Center, Miami; Yongmin Zhu, Los Medanos College; Norma Zorilla, Fresno Pacific College.

Summary of Listening/Speaking Exercises and Activities for Learning Strategies and Language Functions

Chapter	Learning Strategies	Listening Exercises	Speaking Activities
one	• making predictions	• predict content	• role-play: prediction of outcomes
two	• listening for main ideas	• complete outlines	• report the gist
three	• listening for key terms • listening for straw man arguments	• note key terms and definitions • note straw man arguments	• describe a typical day; define key terms • use straw man arguments in interviews and discussion
four	• listening for analogies	• note analogies	• describe a scene using analogies
five	• taking notes on a field trip	• label a process diagram • fill in data on a chart	• use notes to describe a process
six	• listening for pros and cons	• fill in a pro/con chart	• discuss pros and cons of investment options
seven	• listening for chronological order	• fill in a time chart	• order sentences • create a chronological round-robin story
eight	• listening for signal words	• note signal words and their definitions	• discuss various forms of communication
nine	• recognizing digressions	• identify main points and digressions • note phrases introducing digressions	• note and share digressions heard in various contexts • tell stories using digressions
ten	• paraphrasing	• listen to paraphrase main ideas	• paraphrase short readings
eleven	• outlining	• complete an outline	• use an outline to organize thoughts for presentation
twelve	• summarizing	• create minibiographies	• complete the saying • role-play quotes

Language Functions	Listening Exercises	Speaking Activities
• offering and requesting clarification	• identify intentions and expressions	• use expressions with riddles and brain teasers
• asking for confirmation	• identify appropriate expressions	• use expressions to elicit the "truth"
• making generalizations • introducing information	• identify true/false information • recognize surprising information	• discuss general information • share unusual or surprising • events report surprising research
• expressing opinions	• identify personal opinions • complete opinion statements	• role-play: characters with definite views
• shifting focus	• recognize shifts: active to passive; personal to impersonal • complete sentences	• present rationales in active and passive voice • role-play: eyewitness reporting
• agreeing and disagreeing	• identify appropriate ways of agreeing and disagreeing • react to arguments	• agree/disagree with a suggestions or point of view
• expressing likes and dislikes	• recognize subtleties of expressions • note likes and dislikes	• respond to questions • use tone of voice to express likes and dislikes
• divulging information	• identify formal and informal expressions	• complete conversations
• asking for information, seeking confirmation, and challenging with tag questions	• recognize relationship of tone to meaning of tag questions • chart categories of tag questions	• conduct interviews using tag questions • create role-plays using tag questions
• expressing wishes, hopes, and desires	• note expressions of hope and desire • paraphrase hopes and desires	• role-play: hopes and desires • discuss personal wishes/dreams
• stating reasons	• note expressions for stating reasons • complete sentences with appropriate expressions	• present facts, feelings, opinions, and reasons
• telling a joke	• recognize humor introduced by pacing or tone • complete quotations	• discuss funny people • tell jokes • use humor in discussions

A Listening/ Speaking Skills Book

mosaic one

CHAPTER **one**

New Challenges

You will listen to a lecture called "Learning to Speak Someone Else's Language." It might be the first lecture in a basic linguistics course or in a course on communications theory.

Skill A—Learning Strategy: Listening to Make Predictions

Skill B—Language Function: Offering and Requesting Clarification

DID YOU KNOW?

- The person who holds the record for speaking the most languages was Dr. Harold Williams of New Zealand. He was a journalist who lived from 1876 to 1928. He taught himself to speak 58 languages and many dialects fluently.

- The language with the most letters in its alphabet is Khmer, which used to be called Cambodian. It has 74 letters. The language with the shortest alphabet is that of the Rotokas of Papua, New Guinea. They have only 11 letters (*a, b, e, g, i, k, o, p, r, t,* and *u*).

- The most complicated language in the world may be the language spoken by the Inuit peoples of North America and Greenland. It has 63 different types of present tense, and some nouns can have up to 250 different forms.

Getting Started
Sharing Your Experience

Do the following discussion activities in groups of three or four.

activity 1

Someone once said that getting to know a person is like peeling an onion. What do you think about this comparison? Have you ever peeled an onion? What was it like? How might peeling an onion be like getting to know a person?

activity 2

Have you ever had an experience like the following one? You are vacationing or traveling in a place where you do not know anyone. No one knows who you are either. You find yourself behaving differently than "normal." Try to recall an experience like this in detail. Share your memories with two classmates. Include answers to these questions:

1. *Where* were you?
2. *What* did you do?
3. *Why* did you do it?
4. Is it sometimes easier to open up to people who don't know you? Why is this so?

activity 3

Has your study of English changed you in any way? If so, how? For example, has it made you more outgoing? Has it made you more or less critical of how people speak your native language? Has it made you more or less tolerant of other cultures? Has it changed your understanding or opinon of human nature? Share your answers to these questions with your group.

Vocabulary

exercise The italicized words in the following sentences are used in the lecture in this chapter. Choose the best definition for the italicized word or words in each sentence and put the appropriate letter in the space provided.

1. _____ As your lecturer prepared this lecture for you, he looked at the *collage* made of paper, wood, paint, leaves, and glue hanging on the wall of his office.

2. _____ "This all looks so familiar. Are you sure we've never been here before? No? Really? I guess it must just be *déjà vu*."

3. _____ As a professor of *linguistics,* he is interested in the study of

   _____ language *acquisition*.

4. _____ According to your instructor, because language is very complex and not at all straightforward, it presents us with many *paradoxes*.

5. _____ For many years, researchers thought we learned language through

   _____ *imitation* of others and *association* of words.

6. _____ However, Noam Chomsky, a famous linguist, suggested that the ability to learn a language is *innate*.

7. _____ Learning to speak someone else's language can *fundamentally* change us.

8. _____ As we learn to speak someone else's language, we may *transform* our concepts about the world.

a. connection (in the mind)
b. to change the fundamental nature of something
c. an artistic composition of materials and objects pasted over a surface
d. having to do with the foundation; basically
e. the science of language; study of the nature and structure of human speech
f. something overly familiar; a feeling of having had an experience before
g. present at birth; inborn
h. the act of acquiring or obtaining; development
i. statement/situation that presents opposing views as true at the same time
j. modeling one's behavior on the behavior or actions of another

Noam Chomsky, linguistics professor at Massachusetts Institute of Technology

SKILL A

Listening to Make Predictions

Part of the nature of life is that we can never be absolutely sure what will happen next. Surprises can be nice in everyday life, but if they occur frequently when we listen to a lecture, the lecture may seem difficult to understand. In order not to be surprised too often, it is useful to stay one step ahead of the instructor and anticipate what the instructor will say next in the lecture. Here are two guidelines to help you make predictions.

1. Before you listen to the lecture, think about what you already know and what you want to learn about the topic.
   a. What do you already know about the topic Learning to Speak Someone Else's Language?
   b. What do you think the speaker will discuss?
   c. What questions do you have on the topic?

2. As you listen to the lecture, you can make predictions about what the speaker will say. The pattern goes like this:
   a. The lecturer makes a statement.
   b. You predict what she or he will say next.
   c. You judge quickly whether you were right or wrong.
   d. If you were right, move on to your next prediction.
   e. If you were wrong, don't worry about it or you'll miss what's coming next. Just try to understand as much as you can, put a question mark in your notes for clarification later, and move on to the next prediction.

By focusing on a lecture this way, you become more involved. When you are really involved in listening, you are less likely to be distracted by thoughts of things such as lunch, your soccer game, or the date you had Saturday night.

Listen In

Listen to segments of the lecture one at a time. This will give you the opportunity to understand what has been said already and to predict what will come next. The quotes from the lecture indicate where you should stop the tape.

Stop 1   *"Just call out your questions, and I'll write them down on the overhead."*

Predict what questions you think the students will ask.

_____

_____

_____

_____

_____

Stop 2 *". . . let's begin with that last question. Can we ever really learn to speak another person's language?"*

Did you predict some of the questions the students asked? What do you think the professor will say in the next few minutes?

_____

_____

_____

Stop 3 *". . . which brings us back to the first question on our list: Where does language come from? How does it develop?"*

How do you think the professor will answer this question?

_____

_____

_____

Stop 4 *"Chomsky's theories suggest something about the structure, or grammar, of language, but not very much about how language is used."*

Have you ever heard of Chomsky? What do you think he said about language?

_____

_____

_____

Stop 5 *". . . the rules of our native language . . . can actually determine whatever meaning we find in the world."*

What does this mean? How will the professor explain it? What kind of examples do you think he might give?

_____

_____

_____

Stop 6 *"The English language regularly takes in words from other languages to better express a thought or name a thing."*

What are some words that the professor might use as examples here?

_____

_____

_____

exercise 2

Listen to the rest of the lecture and if you wish, listen to the entire lecture again. Then, compare your predictions at each of the stops with those of your

Mosaic One • Listening/Speaking

classmates. Were you able to make accurate predictions? What did you learn from your classmates' predictions?

Speak Out

For each of the scenarios here and on pages 8 to 10, predict what you think will occur. Follow these three rules:

1. Don't tell anyone your predictions.
2. Write what you think will happen in the spaces following each scenario.
3. Include in your predictions whether the characters will communicate well ("speak each other's language") or whether they will have a misunderstanding.

Three possibilities are given as examples for the first scenario.

1. *Character 1:* A short gentleman, about sixty-five years old.

   Character 2: A tall lady, about seventy-five years old.

   Scenario: The lady and gentleman meet in front of the only empty seat on a crowded New York City subway. If the man sits down, he is being impolite. If he stands up, he may fall because he is too short to reach the strap.

   Your prediction:

   example: The woman convinces the man to sit down. They start talking. Both of them miss their stops. They communicate well and agree to get off the subway at the next stop and have coffee together.

   example: The man gives the seat to the woman. When the subway starts suddenly, he falls into her lap. They communicate well and they laugh and say the transit authority should have more subways during rush hour.

   example: The man and woman see the seat at the same moment. They communicate poorly and, while they are arguing, someone else comes along and takes the seat.

2. *Character 1:* An eighteen-year-old rock musician who is kind, gentle, and loves his mother. His father died when he was a small boy.

Character 2: A loving but very conservative mother.

Scenario: The rock musician wants to have his ear(s) pierced, but he only wants to do it with his mother's permission. The mother and son are sitting in the living room discussing the pros and cons of ear piercing.

Your prediction: _____

_____

_____

_____

3. *Character 1:* A shy young man, twenty-five years old.

Character 2: A liberated young woman, twenty-three years old.

Scenario: The young man and young woman met five-and-a-half weeks ago. She would like to marry him. He would like to marry her. They're finishing a romantic dinner at a very nice restaurant. Both the young man and the young woman are trying to figure out a way to bring up the topic of marriage.

Your prediction: _____

_____

_____

_____

_____

_____

_____

_____

_____

4. *Character 1:* A young man named Harry, twenty-two years old, with two tickets to a soccer match.

Character 2: A young man named Bob, twenty-two years old. Bob has a passion for soccer and a chemistry midterm exam tomorrow.

Scenario: Bob and Harry are in the Student Union at 3:00 P.M. They are drinking coffee. Harry is trying to convince Bob to go to the soccer match.

Your prediction: _____

_____

_____

_____

5. *Character 1:* A student.

Character 2: A grocery store clerk, a student and friend of Character 1.

Scenario: The first student is at the checkout stand of the store with $83 worth of soft drinks, pretzels, potato chips, cheese, crackers, beer, and wine for a party. He finds he has only $64 cash with him and no checks. The clerk at the store is a close personal friend of Character 1 but has not yet been invited to the party.

Your prediction: _____

_____

_____

_____

6. *Character 1:* A freshman named Randy at Needles College is not athletic at all and always makes jokes about exercising.

Character 2: A freshman named Sandy at Red River College is very athletic and jogs every day.

Scenario: Before the two young women, Randy and Sandy, who are very good friends, went off to college in September, Randy said: "I bet I'll lose ten pounds by Thanksgiving and you won't." Each young woman placed a secret note that said "If I lose ten pounds and you don't, you have to _____" inside an envelope. Now it is Thanksgiving vacation. First the young women open the envelopes and read the notes. Then they each get on the scale.

Your prediction (be sure to include what each young woman wrote in her secret note): _____

_____

_____

_____

7. *Character 1:* A widowed father living in Chicago.

Character 2: His son, age fifteen.

Scenario: The father has been offered a good position with higher pay in Toronto and wants to move. But his son does not want to leave Chicago, his high school, and all his friends. They are discussing this problem at the breakfast table.

Your prediction: _____

_____

_____

_____

8. *Character 1:* An "A" student who just got a failing grade for the first time on a midterm exam.

Character 2: A professor, about forty years old, who is tough but usually fair.

Scenario: It is the professor's office hour, and the student is explaining why he or she failed the exam. The student tells the professor about a personal problem and asks to take the exam again.

Your prediction: _____

_____

_____

_____

9. *Character 1:* The father of a three-day-old baby.

Character 2: The mother of the baby.

Scenario: The law in the place where the characters live requires that parents choose a name for their baby after three days. The mother wants to name the baby Sunshine; the father hates that name and wants to name the baby Hester, after his mother.

Your prediction: _____

_____

_____

_____

_____

_____

10. *Character 1:* Josephine, an art student who just moved into a new apartment.

Character 2: Rob, a business major and a friend of Josephine's.

Scenario: Josephine is in her new apartment, hanging pictures on the wall. The doorbell rings and Rob walks in with a gift, a picture for Josephine's apartment. Josephine thinks it is the ugliest picture she has ever seen.

Your prediction: _____

_____

_____

_____

 **activity 2** Choose a partner for this role-play activity and follow the steps below.

1. Choose one of the ten scenarios to act out. (More than one pair can choose the same scenario.)
2. Plan your role play with your partner. You may use the prediction that you wrote for the scenario, the one your partner wrote, or a third prediction that you both agree upon as the basis for your "story."
3. When you and your partner are ready (probably in 10 to 12 minutes), present your role play to the class.
4. After each pair of students presents a role play, share the predictions you all wrote about that scenario. Did anyone in the class predict what happened in the role play?
5. Were your predictions similar, or were they all quite different? If there were similarities, why do you think this happened?
6. If there were a variety of different predictions, do you think your individual perspectives (your private languages) account for the differences? Discuss why or why not.

SKILL **B**

Offering and Requesting Clarification

We all have noticed that sometimes people don't seem to be following what we are saying. These listeners might look puzzled, with their eyebrows pulled together, or they might appear tense or nervous as they keep trying to understand. Listeners who are not following what we are saying simply may not be paying attention. If this is the case, we may see a dreamy look in their eyes.

Ways to Offer Clarification

One way to make sure that people will understand what we are saying is to offer clarification when it is needed. To do this we can either repeat the information exactly or say it again in another way (using different words).

Expressions to Offer Clarification

Are you following me?	
Are you with me?	
Did you get that?	
Do you understand so far?	Appropriate for most situations
Does that make sense to you?	
Is that clear?	
Okay, so far?	
Right?	
Did you catch that?	Not appropriate for
Got it?	formal situations

When you use these expressions to check whether or not people need clarification, listeners are usually appreciative. But be careful with your tone of voice. Some of the expressions can easily sound like reprimands, and you'll sound as if you were angry because they weren't listening.

Conversations

Listen to the following speakers. Each of them uses the same expression to try to find out whether the listener is following what has been said.

conversation 1 Mrs. Garcia is talking to a group of employees. Listen to the speaker and answer the questions.

   1. Which of the expressions in the list above does Mrs. Garcia use?

   _____

   2. What is her intention when she uses this expression?

   _____

   _____

conversation 2 Mrs. Smith is talking to her son. Listen to the speaker and answer the question.

   Mrs. Smith uses the same expression as Mrs. Garcia. What is Mrs. Smith's intention when she uses this expression? _____

   _____

   _____

Ways to Request Clarification

When you are the speaker and see that someone isn't following you, it is easy to be polite and offer clarification. When you are the listener, however, you cannot be certain that the speaker will know just when you need clarification. Therefore, when you don't understand what someone is saying, don't wait for clarification. Request information when you need it. This may mean that you will have to interrupt the speaker.

Polite Expressions for Interrupting

ONE OF THESE:	FOLLOWED BY ONE OF THESE:
Could/Can/May I interrupt?	Would you mind repeating that?
Excuse me.	Could/Would you repeat that please?
Pardon me.	Could/Would you say that again please?
I beg your pardon.	I didn't get the last part (word, etc.).
I'm sorry.	What was that again?

In more informal situations, you may use these expressions to request clarification.

Informal Expressions for Requesting Clarification

Huh? (very informal)	What?
I didn't get the last part (word, etc.).	What did you say?
I didn't catch that.	You lost me.

Listen In

When you listened to the lecture earlier, did you notice that the lecturer uses several of the expressions for offering clarification? Using the same expressions repeatedly is part of a lecturer's style. Being familiar with a lecturer's style can help you understand the content more easily.

Listen to the lecture again. As you listen this time, notice which expressions in the list below the lecturer uses to offer clarification. Each time the lecturer uses an expression, put a check (✓) next to it.

Okay, so far? _____

Does that make sense to you? _____

Right? _____

Did you get that? _____

Are you following me? _____

exercise 2

Discuss these questions with your classmates:

1. Which expressions seem to be the professor's favorite ones?
2. Which ones doesn't he use?
3. Did you need clarification when the professor offered it?
4. Were there times when you needed clarification and the professor did not offer it?

exercise 3

Listen to the lecture again.

1. If you are listening to the lecture by yourself, stop the tape whenever you do not understand something and practice requesting clarification. Practice using a variety of the expressions. Put a check next to each expression as you practice it.
2. If you are listening to the lecture during class, raise your hand when you do not understand something. Your instructor will stop the tape, and you may request clarification from the instructor or from a classmate. Again, practice using a variety of expressions. Be ready to help your classmates, if you can, when they request clarification.

Every day many cultures mingle in Central Park, New York City

Speak Out

activity

Choose a partner for this activity. Take turns presenting the following challenging problems to each other. Some of them are riddles and others might be called "brain teasers." As you do them, you'll understand why. (The answers are on page 149.) Proceed with the activity this way:

Step 1 *Presenter:* Read the problem to your partner as quickly as you can. Do not pause at all.

Listener: Keep your book closed. Do not read along with your partner. If you do not understand something and need clarification, tell your partner this. Use one of the expressions in the Skill B section.

Step 2 *Presenter:* Read the problem again. This time, slow down a little and frequently use expressions to check if your partner needs clarification.

Listener: Tell your partner if you still need clarification.

Step 3 *Presenter:* Slow down even more if necessary.

Listener: Try to solve the problem.

When you have done all the problems with your partner, compare your answers with those of your classmates.

1. How much is 1 times 2 times 3 times 4 times 5 times 6 times 7 times 8 times 9 times 0?

2. Write down this eight-digit number: 12,345,679. Multiply this number by any *one* of the eight numbers. Now multiply by 9. What did you get. Try it again, but this time multiply by another of the eight digits before you multiply by 9. What did you get this time?

3. Mary lives on the twelfth floor of her apartment building. When she wants to go to her apartment, she gets into the elevator in the lobby and pushes the button for the sixth floor. When the elevator arrives at the sixth floor, she gets off and walks up the stairs to the twelfth floor. Mary prefers to ride the elevator, so why does she get off and walk up the stairs?

4. Farmer Higg owns three pink pigs, four brown pigs, and one black pig. How many of Higg's pigs can say that they are the same color as another pig on Higg's farm?

5. What is it that occurs once in a minute, twice in a moment, yet not at all in a week?

6. Think of a number from 1 to 20. Add 1 to this number. Multiply by 2. Add 3. Multiply by 2. Subtract 10. Tell me the answer and I'll tell you the number you started with.

7. A man wants to cross a river. He has a lion, a sheep, and a bale of hay that he must take with him. He has a boat, but it will carry only him and one other thing. So the trouble is, if he leaves the lion alone with the sheep, the lion might eat the sheep. If he leaves the sheep alone with the hay, the sheep might eat the hay. How does he get himself, the lion, the sheep, and the hay to the other side of the river?

8. The governor of Goleta wants to give a small dinner party. He invites his father's brother-in-law, his brother's father-in-law, his father-in-law's brother, and his brother-in-law's father. How many people does he invite?

Understanding spoken English on standardized listening comprehension tests (such as the TOEFL) is more difficult than in other contexts. For example, during a standardized test, you cannot interact with the speaker to get clarification or rewind the tape to listen again. You get only one chance to listen for the important information. The Focus on Testing exercises in this book will help you practice this skill.

You will hear two speakers. After each speaker finishes talking, you will hear a question. To answer the question, read the four possible answers and decide which one is the best answer. Circle the letter of the best answer.

SPEAKER 1

A. Why he didn't get the part in the school play.
B. What Dr. Jackson said yesterday.
C. What kind of play a pun is.
D. What Dr. Jackson just said.

SPEAKER 2

A. Some languages are more fun to learn than others.
B. Adults and children speak the same language.
C. Some languages are disappearing from the earth.
D. Children shouldn't speak their parents' native language.

CHAPTER **two**

Looking at Learning

in this chapter

You will listen to a lecture and class discussion in a freshman study skills class. The topic of the lecture is "Learning to Listen/Listening to Learn."

Skill A—Learning Strategy: Listening for the Main Ideas

Skill B—Language Function: Asking for Confirmation

DID YOU KNOW?

- **The largest university in the world is the State University of New York. In 1991 it was composed of 64 campuses across the state and had an enrollment of 400,777 students.**

- **The youngest university student on record is Michael Tan of Christchurch, New Zealand. He was 7 years and 7 months of age when he passed his New Zealand bursary examinations in mathematics, which is equivalent to a high school diploma in the United States. He started study toward a degree in mathematics at Canterbury University, New Zealand, at the age of 7 years and 11 months.**

- **The most expensive school in the world is probably the Gstaad International School in Gstaad, Switzerland. In 1992, the yearly cost was about $55,000.**

Getting Started

Sharing Your Experience

Complete the following discussion activities.

Step 1 Talk about how much time you spend each day doing each of the following: sleeping, speaking, listening, reading, and writing. How much time are you awake but not communicating? On the scale on the top of page 19, indicate how much of each day you think you spend in these activities by placing a check under the appropriate percentage.

Sometimes we listen, sometimes we don't.

Step 2 Compare your scale with those of your classmates. Are the scales similar, or do they vary quite a bit? Discuss the similarities and differences. Share the reasons you marked particular percentages on your scale. Were they similar to your classmates' reasons, or different?

	0%	25%	50%	75%	100%

Sleeping: _____

Speaking: _____

Listening: _____

Reading: _____

Writing: _____

Awake but
not commu-
nicating: _____

 **activity 2**

How fast do you think people speak? Seventy-five words per minute? One hundred twenty-five words per minute? Two hundred? Two hundred seventy-five? Let's find out how fast your teacher and your classmates speak.

Step 1 Your teacher will speak about his or her most memorable learning experience in three intervals of ten seconds each. For each ten-second interval, make a mark (卌,||, etc.) on the lines below for each word your teacher speaks. Then add up all the marks for the three intervals and multiply by 2. This number is the total number of words your teacher might speak in one minute.

Interval 1: _____

Interval 2: _____

Interval 3: _____

Total number of marks _____ × 2 = _____ number of words
spoken per minute

 Step 2 In groups of three, take turns speaking about your most memorable learning experiences. Each student speaks in three intervals of ten seconds each. In the chart below, make a mark for each word your classmates speak in the three intervals. Then add up all the marks and multiply by 2. This gives you the number of words each student might speak in one minute.

	student A	student B	student C
Interval 1	_____	_____	_____
Interval 2	_____	_____	_____
Interval 3	_____	_____	_____
	Total marks ____ × 2 = ____ words per minute	Total marks ____ × 2 = ____ words per minute	Total marks ____ × 2 = ____ words per minute

Step 3 Compare the results in your group with those of other groups in the class. What is the average number of words spoken by a student in one minute? How does this compare to the number of words spoken by your teacher in one minute? Do you think you speak faster in your native language? Do you think native English speakers speak too quickly?

 Here's some good news! People can generally understand more words per minute than they can say in the same amount of time. How many spoken words per minute do you think people can understand? Three hundred words per minute? Four hundred? Mark your guess below. The lecture in this chapter will give you the answer and will also reveal some other interesting things about listening skills and how they can be improved.

I THINK PEOPLE CAN UNDERSTAND _____ SPOKEN WORDS PER MINUTE.

Vocabulary

 Fill in the blanks with the correct forms of the following words.

counterexample	*an example that demonstrates an opposite view*
gist	*main idea*
to stick with	*to keep working on, stay with*
uncomplicated	*simple, easy to understand*
upcoming	*going to happen in the near future*

1. The thing I like about Professor Crawford's lectures is that they are very straightforward and completely _____.

2. I knew the lecturer was wrong because I could easily think of a _____

   _____.

3. What I like about Rose-Marie is that she always _____ her projects and never gives up until they are finished.

4. "I can always get the _____ of what Professor McClellum says, but because of his Scottish accent, I never understand every word," said Julian.

5. I'm really nervous about my _____ exam.

 Share your answers to the following questions with your classmates.

1. "Women are just no good at mathematics. I've never even met a woman who likes math." From your own experience, what is a good counterexample to the previous statement?

2. Think of a film that you saw, either here or in your native country. Briefly, what was the gist of it?

3. Do you think there is a difference between being a "quitter" and knowing when (the right time) to quit? Do you always stick with everything you start? Why or why not?

4. Do you live a complicated or uncomplicated life? To explain your answer, share a few examples.

5. What are one or two upcoming events on your calendar?

Listening for the Main Ideas

Most lectures have a single main idea. It is the one idea that you can state briefly when a classmate asks you, "What was the lecture about?" In most cases, there are several other main ideas in addition to the overall one. These main ideas are the messages that the lecturer most wants you to remember.

Lecturers also present examples and details to back up the main ideas. Facts and illustrations may come before or after the main idea they relate to. It is easier for you to pick out main ideas and understand the lecture as a whole if you can identify the order in which the speaker is presenting main ideas and details.

Guidelines for Listening for Main Ideas

1. As you listen to a lecture, make note of the most important points and try to separate them out from the details and illustrations.

2. Identify whether the lecturer is using the deductive or inductive method of presenting ideas. The deductive method starts with a main idea, followed by several examples or details that support it. The inductive method starts with the details and builds up to the main idea.

DEDUCTIVE	INDUCTIVE
Main Idea 1	Examples or Details 1
Examples or Details 1	Main Idea 1
Main Idea 2	Examples or Details 2
Examples or Details 2	Main Idea 2

3. Lecturers sometimes mix these two ways of presenting information, which can be confusing. If an instructor does this, it is a good idea to rewrite your notes as soon as possible after class so that you can clearly identify the main ideas, separate them out from supporting details, and straighten out anything that is confusing to you.

Listen In

This exercise will help you listen for the main ideas in the lecture. Details are in the left column. Read them first. Then listen to the lecture. As you listen, fill in the main ideas in the right column. The first one has been done for you. You will probably want to listen to the lecture more than once.

DETAILS

A. We can reread, but we cannot relisten to a message.
B. We can control the speed when we read, but we can't when we listen.
C. When we listen we must understand immediately, since we can't use a dictionary easily.

A. Think ahead.
B. Evaluate what the speaker says.
C. Review what has been said.

A. People are less likely to daydream when taking notes.
B. Notes make it easier to review.
C. Notes can remind you of information you have forgotten.

A. Write only "Bee hummingbird is 2½ inches."

A. You can review notes after dinner, before you go to sleep, or the first thing in the morning.

A. Thesis/conclusion system
B. Fact/principle system

MAIN IDEA

1. _Reading and listening are_ _different in three ways._ _____

2. _____ _____ _____ _____

3. _____ _____ _____ _____

4. _____ _____ _____

5. _____ _____ _____ _____

6. _____ _____ _____ _____

Speak Out

In addition to identifying the main ideas during lectures, we must also be able to get the gist of what is said during personal conversations. The main ideas expressed during a personal conversation may be straightforward, uncomplicated statements such as:

- It was fun having the class party at Disneyland this year.
- I really don't like dormitory food.
- I admire my biology professor.

Just as in lectures, this type of statement in conversation is usually followed or preceded by examples and details.

However, the main ideas expressed during a conversation may not always be so straightforward. Sometimes details may be given, but a direct statement connecting these details may not be given. In these cases, the gist of what the person is saying most often has to do with her or his personal feelings or opinions. Then the main idea can be inferred only from these feelings or opinions.

 Consider the following conversation between Keesha and Jared.

JARED: How's the food at the cafeteria here?

KEESHA: Well, the soup is very salty, they cook the vegetables for hours, and the meat is always gray. If they serve it with applesauce, you know that it's pork; if they serve it with mint jelly, it's lamb.

What is the **gist** of what Keesha is saying about the cafeteria food? _____

_____

 **activity 2**

Step 1 For this activity you must find a native English speaker who has done one of the following:

- attended school in a foreign country
- lived in a dormitory
- shared an apartment with other students
- rented a room from a family
- taught a class
- failed (or almost failed) a class
- learned a new skill
- been active in politics
- worked while going to school

Step 2 Ask the person to tell you about this experience. As you listen, make mental notes of the main ideas. Pay close attention in order to get the gist of what the person is saying.

Step 3 Report back to the class about your conversation. Be sure to include the following:

- a brief description of the person you spoke with and the situation you spoke about.
- the main ideas, the gist of the conversation.
- whether the gist of what the person said was stated directly or not.

Step 4 Find out if any of the people you and your classmates spoke with had similar experiences? That is, were any of the main ideas they expressed similar? If so, why do you think this was the case?

SKILL

Asking for Confirmation

Sometimes it is difficult to know exactly what a speaker means, even when you have heard and understood every word. When this happens, you can ask the speaker for confirmation of your understanding. A good way to do this is to state what you heard in your own words and then ask the speaker if you understood correctly.

In the classroom, the situation can be sensitive. You don't want the instructor to feel that you think he or she explains things badly. This might make the instructor feel insulted or angry. To confirm that you have understood without insulting the instructor, you must ask your questions carefully. Page 25 shows some polite expressions you might use.

With friends or family you can confirm something less formally by omitting the first sentence and using only one of the second sentences listed. Or you may simply ask, "You mean . . . ?"

Conversations

Listen to the following conversations. Expressions to ask for confirmation are used correctly in some conversations and incorrectly in others. Sometimes the intonation makes the difference.

At the side of the road, a lost driver is asking a police officer for directions. Listen to the speakers and answer the question. Then discuss your answer with your classmates.

Did the lost driver ask for confirmation appropriately? _____

Here is a conversation between a professor and a student. Listen to the speakers and answer the question. Discuss your answer with your classmates.

Did the student respond appropriately? _____

Here is a similar conversation between the same professor and student. Listen to the speakers and answer the question.

1. How do you feel about this student's confirmation strategy?

_____

_____

2. Do your classmates feel the same way? Ask them.

In this conversation, a student is talking to a secretary about the preregistration procedure. Listen to the speakers and answer the questions. Share your answers with your classmates.

Would you react the same way if you were this secretary? _____

Why or why not? _____

 Here is another conversation between a secretary and a student. Listen to the speakers and answer the question. Discuss this with your classmates.

What is the critical element that makes the difference between conversations 4 and 5? _____

_____

_____

_____

Listen In

Now listen to the lecture again. This time your instructor will stop the tape so that you can ask for confirmation of your understanding. Read the following sentences before you listen to the tape. These are the last sentences you will hear before your instructor stops the tape. Each time the instructor stops the tape, several of you should practice asking for confirmation using the appropriate expressions. The first item is done for you.

Stop 1   *"One-half of that time was spent listening."*
Do you mean that 50 percent of the time was spent listening?

Stop 2   *"When we listen, the rate or speed of the message is established by the speaker."*

Stop 3   *"Actually, people can listen at a rate of 300 words per minute and not lose any comprehension."*

Stop 4   *"Now he's going to talk about Newton's ideas on motion from Chapter 2 because he's already finished talking about Galileo from Chapter 1."*

Stop 5   *"Or you may decide to do it the last thing at night before you go to sleep—or the first thing in the morning."*

Stop 6 *"The thesis/conclusion system works best with well-organized lectures that have an introduction, a body, and a conclusion."*

Stop 7 *"Then, when you review, you can see if the principles tie together into one main concept or thesis."*

Stop 8 *"And believe me, you'll get plenty of chances to practice all of this throughout the term."*

Speak Out

Have you ever given an excuse that was not the truth for something you forgot or did not want to do? Did the other person believe you? Or did the other person question what you said? Consider these examples:

STUDENT: I'm sorry I don't have my homework, but my dog ate it.

TEACHER: I'm not sure I understand. Do you mean to say that your dog likes to eat paper?

YOUNG WOMAN: No, I can't go to the movies with you. I have to wash my hair.

YOUNG MAN: I don't get it. You mean you wash your hair every night?

Notice how the teacher challenges the student in the first example, and the young man challenges the young woman in the second. They don't actually say the other person is lying, but it is clear that they suspect this. However, even by challenging the student and young woman, the teacher and the young man may not get the truth. By asking for confirmation in a gentle tone of voice, you may be able to get at the truth and still be polite.

 For this activity, do the following nine steps. Then present one of your role-plays.

1. Choose a partner.
2. Make an excuse for something you forgot or don't want to do (for example, returning books to the library, going to the opera, or cleaning up the kitchen). Your excuse may be real or made up.
3. Your partner should question the truth of this excuse, using an expression asking for confirmation.
4. Then answer this question with another excuse (either real or entirely made up).
5. Your partner should question this excuse too!
6. Answer with an even better excuse.
7. Your partner should question it, and so forth.
8. See how long you can keep making excuses. Then change roles.
9. Later change partners and try it again.

Following is an example of how it might go.

STUDENT: I'm sorry I don't have my homework, but my dog ate it.

TEACHER: I'm not sure I understand. Do you mean to say that your dog likes to eat paper?

STUDENT: Well, yes he does, actually—some sort of vitamin deficiency, I think.

TEACHER: I'm not following this. Are you telling me that paper has nutritional value?

STUDENT: You see, when he was a puppy he was taken away from his mother too soon and . . .

TEACHER: Wait—am I right? Do you mean to tell me that you don't have your homework because your dog had an unhappy childhood? . . .

activity 2

Do this activity in small groups. Imagine that you have completed your education and have a wonderful job in the research and development department of a large company. The other members of your group work there too. You have just invented a new product. Decide as a group what that product is, what it does, how it works, and so forth. Examples are:

- a wristwatch-TV that can be blown up like a balloon to become a ten-inch TV
- an electromagnetic device that can be attached to your tongue to help you pronounce English perfectly

Next, take turns with the other groups describing your strange but wonderful products. When you are listening, interrupt in order to clarify the descriptions of these unusual items. When your group is speaking, be ready to answer any and all questions about *your* product.

focus on testing

You will hear two speakers. After each speaker finishes talking, you will hear a question. Then read the four possible answers and decide which one is the best answer. Circle the letter of the best answer.

SPEAKER 1

A. Frank is not strong enough.
B. Frank is taking too many courses for his first semester.
C. First-year students usually take this many courses.
D. Frank has a lot of different interests.

SPEAKER 2

A. She is tired and hungry.
B. She doesn't want to use the meal plan on weekends.
C. She thinks the meal plan is too expensive for what she is getting.
D. She can't buy food on weekends.

CHAPTER **three**

Relationships

You will listen to a two-part lecture called "Family Networks and the Elderly."
It covers the first two meetings of an undergraduate seminar on this topic.

Skill A—Learning Strategy: Listening for Key Terms

Skill B—Language Function: Making Generalizations

Skill C—Learning Strategy: Listening for "Straw Man" Arguments

Skill D—Language Function: Introducing Information

- **The longest marriage on record lasted 86 years. It was between Sir Temulji Bhicaji Nariman and Lady Nariman, who were wed in 1853 when they were 5 years old.**

- **Adam Borntrager of Medford, Wisconsin, had 675 living descendants. They were: 11 children, 115 grandchildren, 529 great-grandchildren, and 20 great-great-grandchildren.**

- **In the United States, life expectancy is 75.4 years for men and 78.8 years for women.**

Getting Started

Sharing Your Experience

activity

As a class or in small groups, discuss the following questions.

1. What do you know about the treatment of the elderly in the United States or Canada? Do the majority of older people live with their children and grandchildren or by themselves? Do the elderly, in general, live far from or near their children? What distance would you consider far? What distance would you consider near?

2. What do you think the daily life of a sixty-five-year-old person in the United States is like? If you know any elderly people in the United States, describe them. How old are they? What is daily life like for those persons?
3. What is life like for an elderly person in your home country? Use the questions in Activity 1 to guide your discussion.
4. Would you rather grow old in the United States or in your home country? Why?

Vocabulary

As you know, many words have more than one meaning. The definitions of the following vocabulary words match the way the words are used in the lecture.

alienated	*to feel removed, not associated with family or friends*
assumption	*an idea that is understood to be correct*
to favor	*to like best*
household	*people living under one roof, often a family living together*
left	*remaining*
network	*a system of connections*

Complete the following sentences with the correct forms of the vocabulary words.

1. The young boy on the bus gave his seat to the elderly woman because there weren't any other seats _____.

2. The old man felt _____ when none of the young people wanted to listen to his story.

3. There are five people, including a grandparent, in the Smith _____.

4. The elderly couple _____ the apartment on the lower floor because it was not easy for them to climb the stairs any more.

5. In many cities there is a _____ of volunteers who provide assistance to the elderly.

6. We shouldn't make the _____ that all elderly people are sickly or that all young people are healthy.

In small groups, discuss the following questions.

1. Have you ever felt *alienated*? If so, under what circumstances?
2. What *assumptions* did you make about college life before you got to college? How accurate were they?
3. Which would you *favor:* all your classes in the morning or in the afternoon?
4. How many people live in your *household*?
5. How many hours of classes do you have *left* this week?
6. What *network* would you use if you wanted to get someone to introduce you to the president or director of your school?

Listening for Key Terms

Terms that an instructor defines in a lecture are called *key terms.* Key terms are:

- usually new to most students or are used in a new way in the course
- often used to describe the most important concepts in a lecture
- usually defined at the beginning of a lecture or when the instructor begins a new topic
- often appear as test items on exams

Listen In

The lecture in this chapter is divided into two parts. It is designed to give you practice in listening for key terms.

 Listen to part 1 of the lecture. Listen for the words the instructor defines. Write down any key terms the instructor uses.

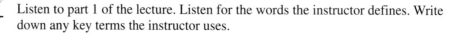

_____

_____

_____

_____

_____

exercise 2 Listen to part 1 of the lecture again. This time, write a brief definition next to each key term. When you have finished, compare your list of key terms and definitions with those of your classmates.

KEY TERM	DEFINITION
_____	_____
	_____
	_____
	_____
_____	_____
	_____
	_____
_____	_____
	_____
	_____
_____	_____
	_____
	_____
_____	_____
	_____
	_____
_____	_____

Speak Out

In small groups, practice defining and listening for key terms. Describe a typical day at home with your family. In the United States and Canada, this is usually a Saturday or a Sunday. You may use some words from your native language if they do not translate easily into English or if you do not yet know the exact translation in English. Such terms might include an unusual food or custom, a game, a type of clothing, or an idiomatic expression.

Follow these rules:

- As you speak, be sure to define any words in your native language that you use. These are key terms.
- As you listen, note the words your classmates define (the key terms) on the chart on page 34. If you don't understand something, ask the person to define it again. You may find the expressions for asking for clarification or confirmation useful here. (See Chapter One, Skill B, page 13, and Chapter Two, Skill B, page 25.)

classmate	key terms	definitions
_____	_____ _____ _____ _____	_____ _____ _____ _____ _____
_____	_____ _____ _____ _____	_____ _____ _____ _____ _____
_____	_____ _____ _____ _____	_____ _____ _____ _____ _____
_____	_____ _____ _____	_____ _____ _____ _____ _____

SKILL B

Making Generalizations

When we make statements about things that can be counted, we try to be accurate. For example:

Of the 100 elderly people who were interviewed, 15 preferred to live with their children and grandchildren, 80 preferred to live alone, and 5 did not have a preference.

However, sometimes we may not know exact numbers. We cannot be accurate, but we do have some general ideas or opinions. In these cases we can describe what we think happens most of the time. We can make generalizations.

Generalizations usually contain adverbs of time and expressions such as these:

by and large	in general
for the most part	normally
generally	typically
generally speaking	usually
hardly ever	seldom
rarely	

Consider these examples:

- By and large, elderly people in the United States prefer to live alone.
- Typically, however, they enjoy visiting with relatives.
- Rock concerts are hardly ever performed in homes for the elderly.
- For the most part, rock concerts are not performed in homes for the elderly.

activity Work in groups of three or four. Discuss whether the two sentences above about rock concerts have about the same meaning. Tell why they do or don't mean the same thing.

Listen In

Listen to part 1 of the lecture again. Pay special attention to how the instructor uses some of the expressions listed in the Skill B section.

Step 1 Mark the following statements T (true) or F (false) as you listen.

Step 2 When you are finished, compare your answers with those of your classmates. Listen to the tape as many times as necessary to check your answers.

Step 3 Finally, in small groups, take turns changing each false statement to a true one by omitting the generalization and adding an appropriate adverb.

1. _____ People over sixty-five are always called elderly.

2. _____ There are only two types of families: nuclear and extended.

3. _____ By and large, a man and his wife and children are the members of what we call a nuclear family.

4. _____ In extended families, married couples rarely live with their parents.

5. _____ Generally, in Africa and Japan, people choose to live in extended families.

6. _____ In many countries, people generally choose to live only with the nuclear family.

7. _____ One assumption many people make is that, generally speaking, elderly people see their children on a regular basis.

8. _____ Another assumption many people make is that elderly people hardly ever see their siblings.

Speak Out

Divide into groups of three to six people. Discuss family life in the United States and in your home country with the other members of your group. You may want to discuss such things as the age when people marry, the average number of people in a household, the number of children in the average family, the divorce rate, the number of single parent families, where the elderly live, who is responsible for earning money, and who is responsible for household chores. Use appropriate expressions for making generalizations.

Handout   Sociology Seminar 270

THE ELDERLY IN THE UNITED STATES

TABLE 1 ELDERLY LIVING WITH CHILDREN OR WITHIN TEN MINUTES BY CAR: THE UNITED STATES AND SELECTED EUROPEAN COUNTRIES

Denmark	52%
United States	61%
Great Britain	66%
Poland	70%
Yugoslavia	73%

TABLE 2 FREQUENCY OF ELDERLY PERSONS' VISITS WITH THEIR CHILDREN

Within 24 Hours		Last Week	
Great Britain	47%	Yugoslavia	71%
Yugoslavia	51%	Poland	77%
United States	52%	Great Britain	77%
Denmark	53%	United States	78%
Poland	64%	Denmark	80%

TABLE 3 PERCENTAGE OF ELDERLY WHO SAW A SIBLING WITHIN THE PAST WEEK

Women		Men	
Poland	37%	Great Britain	28%
Denmark	58%	Denmark	32%
Yugoslavia	40%	Poland	33%
Great Britain	41%	United States	34%
United States	43%	Yugoslavia	48%

Adapted from Ethel Shanas, "Family-Kin Networks and Aging in Cross-Cultural Perspective." *Journal of Marriage and the Family*, August 1973, pp. 508-509. Copyrighted 1973 by the National Council on Family Relations, Fairview Community School Center, 1910 West County Road B, Suite 147, Saint Paul, Minnesota 55113. Reprinted by permission.

SKILL C

Listening for "Straw Man" Arguments

If you were to fight with someone made of straw, you most likely would win. Thus, a "straw man" argument is an argument that can be defeated easily.

Many straw man arguments are based on assumptions people have made that are not true. Many professors feel that part of their job is to help students look objectively at their beliefs and the assumptions they might have made.

Therefore, instructors will often use straw man arguments in their lectures. For example, they will make a statement from one point of view (the straw man argument), and later they will demonstrate why this point of view is not accurate (defeat the argument).

Listen In

Listen to part 2 of the lecture. Listen for the straw man arguments and why they are untrue. As you listen, look at the handout on the Elderly in the United States on page 37. You will probably need to listen to the lecture more than once. Below, fill in information about some of the arguments as you listen. Discuss your answers with classmates.

Straw man argument 1: _____

_____

_____

Information used to defeat argument 1: _____

_____

_____

Straw man argument 2: _____

_____

_____

Information used to defeat argument 2: _____

_____

_____

Straw man argument 3: _____

_____

_____

Information used to defeat argument 3: _____

_____

_____

Straw man argument 4: _____

_____

_____

Information used to defeat argument 4: _____

_____

_____

Speak Out

activity **1**

Step 1 Divide into groups of five or six. Then choose one of the following questions.

What do you think it's like to:

- grow old?
- be a single parent?
- have teenaged children?
- live with your spouse's parents?
- be married and have no children?
- be married, have small children, and work?
- live alone as a young person?
- live alone as an old person?

It's all right if more than one person chooses the same question. Also, it will be more interesting if you choose a situation that you have not experienced yet.

Step 2 Take about two minutes to think about the question you have chosen. Think about what daily life is like for the person in this situation. If you have not had the same experience, you will have to make some assumptions about that person's daily life.

Step 3 Share your assumptions with the rest of your group. Did anyone in your group disagree with your assumptions? Could anyone in the group show that your assumptions were not accurate? How? Discuss any straw man arguments that came up as you talked.

activity **2**

Step 1 Interview someone in the community who is currently in the situation you selected in Activity 1. Ask about the person's daily life. Remember to ask about some of the assumptions you made.

Step 2 Share with the class what happened during the interview. Did any of your assumptions turn out to be straw man arguments? Discuss which ones, and why.

Introducing Information

When we introduce new material or points during a talk, we usually try to prepare the listener in some way.

Expressions for Introducing Expected Information

    Let's consider . . .
    Let's examine . . .
    Let's look at . . .
    Let's reexamine . . .

Expressions for Introducing Surprising Information (Formal)

Believe it or not . . .	Surprisingly . . .
In fact . . .	This is hard to believe, but . . .
Let's face it . . .	You may be surprised that . . .
Oddly enough . . .	You may not (won't) believe this, but . . .

Expressions for Introducing Surprising Information (Informal)

    Do you (ya) know what?
    Guess what!
    Surprise!

Conversations

Listen to the following conversations for examples of expressions used to introduce surprising information.

Mark tells Connie something surprising about his grandfather. Listen to the speakers and answer the question.

Which expressions does Mark use to introduce the surprising information?

_____

_____

conversation 2   Uncle George and his niece, Gina, exchange some surprising information. Listen to the speakers and answer the question.

Which expressions do Uncle George and Gina use to introduce their surprises?

_____

_____

Listen In

exercise 1   Listen to part 2 of the lecture again. List the points that the instructor thinks are surprising.

_____

_____

_____

_____

_____

_____

_____

_____

Speak Out

activity 1   Think of an experience that happened in your family (or in someone else's) that was unusual because the results were very unexpected. Share these experiences in small groups. Use the expressions in Skill D to introduce the surprising points. For example:

Once my family and I went on a picnic in Golden Gate Park in San Francisco. I put my purse down on the grass. Later on everyone went for a walk. We came back two hours later. Believe it or not, my purse was still on the grass. In fact . . .

activity

Step 1 Call a Medicare office, a home for the elderly, a county hospital, or an elderly friend and ask about benefits for the elderly.

Step 2 Report this information (in small groups or to the whole class). Use the expressions in Skill D to introduce surprising points.

focus on testing

You will hear two speakers. After each speaker finishes talking, you will hear a question. To answer the question, read the four possible answers and decide which one is the best answer. Circle the letter of the best answer.

SPEAKER 1

A. Dad is giving his boss a really big present this week.
B. Ruth and James have to do their own homework this week.
C. Ruth and James need to practice pitching for the baseball game.
D. Ruth and James need to help around the house more than usual.

SPEAKER 2

A. He's explaining why he wants to take the dog along on vacation.
B. He's explaining why they have to leave the dog home this year.
C. He's trying to convince them to visit the Grand Canyon.
D. He's saying that they have to stay home to take care of the dog this summer.

CHAPTER four

Health

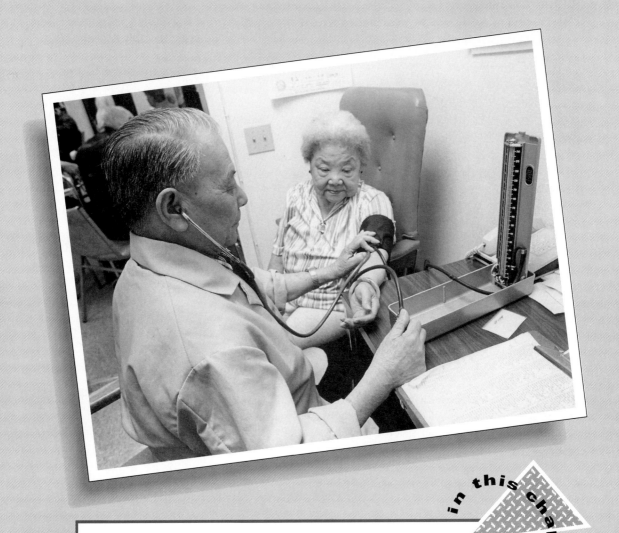

You will listen to a study session where three students are reviewing their notes on a lecture about the heart. The title of the lecture they are discussing is "What Makes Us Tick: The Cardiac Muscle."

Skill A—Learning Strategy: Listening for Analogies

Skill B—Language Function: Expressing Opinions

DID YOU KNOW?

- The heart rate for cold-blooded animals varies with the temperature in the environment.

- Most people's hearts beat about 75 times a minute. But this rate can go to over 200 beats a minute for a short time when the body is working hard.

- A clam's heart rate varies from 2 to 20 beats per minute. What could a clam be doing to get its heart rate up to 20 beats per minute?

Getting Started
Sharing Your Experience

As a class or in small groups, do the following discussion activity.

The human body is often compared to a machine. In what ways is the human body like the machines listed below? Consider specific organs as you discuss these questions.

example: a camera

The eye is like an automatic camera. It automatically focuses for short and long distances and automatically adjusts for lighting conditions.

1. a car
2. a robot
3. a boat
4. a furnace
5. a computer
6. a telephone switchboard
7. a video recorder
8. a garbage disposal
9. a printing press
10. a telephone answering machine
11. a laptop computer

Vocabulary

The speakers in this chapter use the following words as they describe the heart.

chambers	*compartments*
hollow	*having an empty space inside*
overall	*in general, including everything*
peel	*outside covering of some fruits, such as bananas*
to pump	*to propel or push*
strip	*long, narrow piece*
ticktock	*the sound a clock makes*
undoubtedly	*unquestionably, without any doubt*
to vary	*to change, differ*
canary	*a small yellow bird*

 **exercise**

Complete the following sentences with the correct forms of the vocabulary words.

1. Anthony Robbins, who runs fourteen miles every day, _____ has the strongest heart in the class.

2. The _____ in the heart fill and empty as the heart works.

3. The _____ of the clock reminded Diana of her own heartbeat.

4. Jane's mother bought her a _____ to try to cheer her up after her recent heartbreak.

5. The heart _____ the blood through the body.

6. Ruben's health is, _____ , quite good.

7. You can use the _____ of an orange to make some healthy drinks.

8. Francis used a _____ of cloth to make a bandage.

9. The size of an animal's heart _____ according to the size of the rest of its body.

SKILL **A**

Listening for Analogies

When instructors explain a new concept to their students, they often compare the new idea to something that is already familiar to them. For example, the human body is said to be like a machine, and the eye may be said to be like a camera. These comparisons are called *analogies*.

Listen In

Listen to the study session on the tape once all the way through. Then listen to the session again and write down all the analogies you hear. You can write them in short form, as in the following examples.

> **examples:**   body = machine
>
>   eye = camera

_____

_____

_____

_____

_____

_____

 Share your list of analogies with your classmates. If others wrote down more analogies than you did, listen to the study session once more and see how many more analogies you can discover.

Speak Out

You have just heard a study session that included many analogies. Using analogies in your conversation can make what you say clearer, more interesting, and even poetic. In this activity you will have the opportunity to describe actions, feelings, and objects by making analogies.

 On the facing page, seven situations are outlined. For each set of circumstances, think about how the people might feel. Try to imagine:

- what they are doing with their hands
- what they are doing with their eyes
- what they are doing with their bodies
- what objects they are holding or looking at
- how you would feel in the same situation

With a classmate, choose one of the situations and pantomime it for the rest of the class. Don't talk. Just present a brief silent scene and let your classmates describe your feelings and actions by making analogies. An example is provided for the first situation.

1. *In the dentist's office:* The patient is extremely fearful. The dentist is confident and reassuring.

   While you and your partner are portraying the scene, your classmates might offer analogies about the characters, such as the following:

   THE PATIENT

   His hand is shaking like a leaf.
   His face is white as a sheet.
   His mouth feels just like dry desert air.
   His skin feels as cold as a fish.
   His stomach is tied in knots.
   His heart is pounding like a drum.
   He is sweating bullets.
   He feels as scared as a rabbit.

   THE DENTIST

   He feels as solid as a rock.
   His heart is ticking like a quiet clock.
   He has a smile like a well-fed baby's.
   His eyes are calm, like a lake on a windless day.
   His legs are steady, just like two oak trees.
   His touch is as comforting as a soft blanket.
   His hands move precisely, just like an expert watchmaker's.

2. *In the hospital:* The patient is just waking up after an operation. The nurse is new on the job and taking care of a patient for the first time.

3. *At the health club:* The member did too much exercise on the exercise equipment and is now in extreme pain. The director is nervous because other members might think that there's something wrong with the program or with the equipment.

4. *In the woods:* A couple is backpacking for the first time. It's getting dark, they haven't eaten, it's starting to rain, and they can't figure out how to put up the tent.

5. *At home:* A child who doesn't want to go to school pretends to be sick. The mother knows the child is not really sick.

6. *At the office:* The boss is giving a long, uninteresting talk on sales data for the month. An employee who should be listening is thinking about an upcoming ski trip.

7. *In the school cafeteria:* Two students are eating lunch.

SKILL **B**

Expressing Opinions

In the study session in this chapter, the speakers present a lot of factual information. In addition to these facts, the speakers express many personal opinions. In general, when people want to express personal opinions, they use specific expressions to introduce them. These expressions help the listener distinguish the facts from information that may be only personal beliefs.

Expressions Used to Introduce Personal Opinions

I bet . . .	I'm pretty sure . . .
I'd say . . .	I personally think . . .
I guess . . .	I strongly believe . . .
I imagine . . .	I suspect . . .
I'm almost positive . . .	I think . . .
I'm convinced . . .	Not everyone will agree with me, but . . .
I'm fairly certain . . .	To my mind . . .
I'm positive . . .	Undoubtedly . . .

Conversations

In most instances we do not want to mislead other people, nor do we want to sound like "know-it-alls"—people who say that *they* know the facts or the truth but who are frequently proved to be wrong later on. Listen to the following conversations, in which two people express their opinions.

conversation 1 Here is a brief debate between Joe and Paul. Listen to the speakers and answer the questions.

   1. Does Joe express an opinion? _____

   2. Does Paul express an opinion?_____

   3. Does Paul indicate that his is a personal opinion?_____

   4. Which person sounds like a know-it-all?_____

     Why? _____

conversation 2 Let's give Joe and Paul another chance. Listen to the speakers and answer the question.

   What expressions does Paul use this time to introduce his personal opinions?

_____

_____

Listen In

Listen to the study session again. This time, focus on the expressions used to express opinions. Then read the items below. Each item relates to an opinion. Add the missing information to each item, using your own words if you wish.

example: One student is convinced that the cardiac muscles are

the most amazing muscles in the human body.

1. According to Professor Miller, it is the action of the cardiac muscles that _____

   _____ .

2. Fred is positive that the heart looks like _____

   _____ .

3. He says that the top walls of the heart are about the thickness of _____

   _____ .

4. Professor Miller was pretty sure that if the students opened and closed their hands thirty-eight times in half a minute, their hands _____

   _____ .

5. Fred suspects that, generally, the heart beats faster when

   _____

   _____ .

6. One student is convinced that scientists will know more about the

   _____

   _____ in ten or fifteen years.

7. Tory says that the heart works _____

   _____ .

8. One student imagines that the heart rests because _____

   _____ .

9. She personally thinks that one day people will be able to get heart repairs as easily as _____

   _____ .

10. Does this student believe that everyone will agree with her opinion about heart repairs? _____

Speak Out

Divide into groups of five to seven. Discuss the following three situations. Use the expressions in the Skill B section to introduce your personal opinions. If you wish, discuss other situations related to health.

SITUATION 1

The office workers in an insurance company did not do well on the yearly physical examination. They must decide what can be done to improve their physical fitness. They hold a meeting to discuss this.

CHARACTERS

the owner of the company
an extremely overweight secretary
the company doctor, who smokes
the company nurse, who is a "health nut"
a young executive, who jogs to work

SITUATION 2

Should sex education be taught in school? If so, at what level (elementary, secondary, college) and in what class (health, biology, physical education)? A school meeting is held to discuss this issue.

CHARACTERS

a conservative parent
a broad-minded or liberal parent
a school principal
a high school senior
a counselor

SITUATION 3

It is now public law in most states that smoking is not allowed in classrooms, courthouses, and other public buildings. Some cities have

passed laws banning smoking in places such as banks, restaurants, and shopping malls. Many people are hoping that smoking will soon be banned in all workplaces. Do you think the government should be involved in this decision, or should it be left up to the managers or employees or both to decide? A company meeting is held to discuss this issue.

CHARACTERS

an office worker who doesn't smoke but must work in a room with many
    smokers
a student who enjoys smoking
a pregnant woman who becomes ill from the smell of cigarette smoke
a person with a lung disease
an elderly person who has smoked since the age of fifteen

activity **2**

In the same groups, role play the situations in Activity 1. Divide the roles among the group. If you like, add characters of your own or make up another role-play situation related to health. Perform your situations for the class.

You will hear two speakers. After each speaker finishes talking, you will hear a question. To answer the question, read the four possible answers and decide which one is the best answer. Circle the letter of the best answer.

SPEAKER 1

A. We should pass more laws on smoking.
B. People have a right to smoke if they want to.
C. People dying of cancer should be allowed to eat where they want to.
D. People should quit smoking at home and smoke in restaurants instead.

SPEAKER 2

A. She could win a bet on how much weight she can lose.
B. She is overweight like most Americans.
C. She needs to take less luggage on the plane.
D. Most people in America read newspapers.

CHAPTER five

High Tech, Low Tech

in this chapter

You will go on a field trip to the Lyndon B. Johnson Space Center in Houston, Texas, with Professor Chapman and his aeronautics class. You will listen as a guide describes a space flight demonstration called "Space Flight: A Simulation."

Skill A—Learning Strategy: Taking Notes on a Field Trip

Skill B—Language Function: Shifting Focus

DID YOU KNOW?

- **The success of high-tech endeavors can sometimes depend on low-tech strategies. During a space mission to close the doors on the Hubble Space Telescope, all the astronaut's high-tech repair tools failed. They finally just used their own strength to close the doors by hand.**

- **Astronauts F. Story Musgrave and Jeffrey Hoffman needed to replace Hubble's outdated camera with a new one. To protect the camera from damage by the sunlight, they did the job at night using only the two flashlights on their helmets and a couple more that the other astronauts shined out from the windows of the space shuttle *Endeavour*.**

- **When Kathryn Thornton inserted COSTAR, the device that compensates for the Hubble's flawed mirror, she couldn't see what she was doing all the time. Her co-worker, Tom Akers, had to call out directions as she backed COSTAR into its parking place.**

Astronaut Kathryn Thornton in space

Getting Started
Sharing Your Experience

Divide into two groups for five-minute discussions. Each group should choose a secretary to take notes and to give a short report to the class when the discussions are through.

activity **1**

One group's task is to come up with five things the government should spend money on instead of the space program. The other group's job is to list five fields of study not related to the space program that have benefited from space exploration.

After each group has given its report, discuss together the issue of whether a "superpower" or any other country can afford to fund a space program. Give everyone a chance to express their views, regardless of which group they were in originally.

Launch of the *Endeavour*

Vocabulary

The words in the following list are used in the guide's description of the simulation at the Johnson Space Center.

acceleration	*process of going faster*
altitude	*distance above sea level*
astronauts	*people who fly spaceships*
atmosphere	*air surrounding the earth*
cargo bay	*an area in an airplane or spaceship used to keep cargo, special goods, or materials*
external	*on the outside (opposite of internal, on the inside)*
friction	*the rubbing of one thing against another, resistance to motion by two surfaces that are touching*
to manipulate	*to control*
mission	*job*
navigational	*concerning the control or steering of a ship, airplane, or spaceship*
to orbit	*to travel around a body in space (such as the earth)*
orbiter	*a vehicle or thing that orbits*
remote	*distant, far*
satellite	*an object or vehicle made or built to orbit the earth or another body in space*
(to) shuttle	*(v.) to travel back and forth frequently; (n.) a vehicle used to shuttle*
to simulate	*to copy the appearance or effect of something*
solar	*of or about the sun*

 Complete the following sentences with correct forms of the vocabulary terms. There may be more than one correct answer.

1. _____ need a lot of training before they can be put in charge of a flight.

2. Although the scientist was on earth and the spaceship was 690 miles above earth, it was his _____ to repair the ship by _____ control.

3. In order to help the average person understand space exploration better, TV artists _____ the movement of rocket ships on the TV screen.

4. The horrified pilot found it was impossible to _____ the _____ instruments in order to steer the plane.

5. The suitcases were held in the _____ of the plane.

6. As a spaceship enters the earth's _____ at an _____ of 400,000 feet, a great deal of resistance or _____ builds up.

7. They shot up a _____ to _____ the moon; the _____ worked perfectly.

8. There is a bus that will _____ passengers from the airport parking lot to the terminals.

9. On the outside of the spaceship you will find _____ panels, which collect the energy from the sun.

10. As the rockets fired, the _____ of the spaceship pushed the pilots into their seats.

Taking Notes on a Field Trip

It is difficult to take good notes on a field trip. Often, so much material is presented that students can become confused. Here are three hints to help you feel more confident about taking notes on a field trip.

1. Get as much information as possible about the place you are going to visit before the field trip. The more you already know, the easier it will be for you to understand what your guide tells you. You can read a book, look in an encyclopedia, or talk to other students, who have been on a similar field trip.

2. Write down important numbers. Even if you don't have time to write down all the necessary information concerning all the numbers, you can always ask the guide or your instructor to help you fill in the missing information later.

3. Share notes with a friend. You probably won't be able to get every important thing that is said into your notes. Plan to get together with a friend after the field trip to compare notes. Doing this will relieve some anxiety so that you can relax and listen well.

Listen In

Before the space flight simulation, the guide at the Johnson Space Center hands out a diagram of the phases of the space mission you will participate in.

Step 1 Look at the diagram below and the list of coded headings. Before you listen to the space flight simulation on the tape, think about which codes might match the pictures in the diagram.

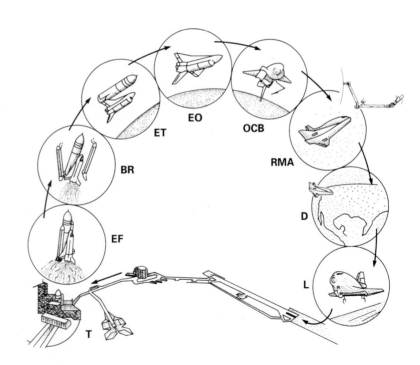

T	=	Tower
OCB	=	Opening Cargo Bay
D	=	Deorbit
EF	=	Engines Fire
BR	=	Booster Rockets Drop Away
EO	=	Enter Orbit (altitude 690 miles)
ET	=	External Tank Drops Away
L	=	Landing
RMA	=	Using Remote Manipulation Arm

Step 2 Now listen to the simulation. As you hear about each phase of the mission in space, label each picture with the appropriate code. The first one is done as an example.

Step 3 Take notes about the Remote Manipulation Arm. Draw or write on the diagram of the arm in the figure below.

Orbiter

Remote Manipulation Arm (R.M.A.)

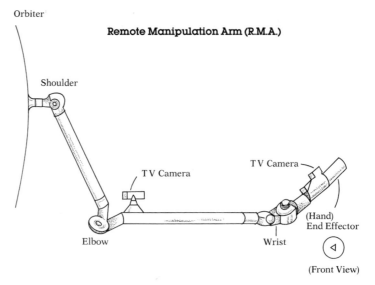

Shoulder

T V Camera

T V Camera

(Hand)
End Effector

Elbow

Wrist

(Front View)

 **Step 1** Now that you have a clearer idea of the technical vocabulary used in the simulation, it will be easier to concentrate on the numbers and statistics. However, you might want to "warm up" by practicing saying the following numbers (and variations of them) aloud with a partner. Make sure you can each identify the numbers spoken.

10	=	ten
100	=	one hundred
1,000	=	one thousand
10,000	=	ten thousand
100,000	=	one hundred thousand
1,000,000	=	one million
10,000,000	=	ten million
100,000,000	=	one hundred million
1,000,000,000	=	one billion
1/2	=	one half
1/3	=	one third
1/4	=	one fourth
1/10	=	one tenth

Step 2   Read items 1 to 10 below. Then listen to the simulation again and fill in the blanks with the correct answers. Go over your answers with a partner.

1. The spaceship's acceleration builds up to _____ feet per second as we move away from the earth.

2. The booster rockets use up their fuel and drop into the sea about _____ minutes after takeoff.

3. As the spaceship goes into orbit, its speed is _____ times the speed of sound.

4. When the spaceship is in orbit, it flies at an altitude of _____ miles.

5. The fifty-foot mechanical arm attached to the orbiter is called the _____ .

6. The area where the satellite will be repaired is called the _____ .

7. The shuttle enters the earth's atmosphere at _____ feet.

8. As the shuttle begins to deorbit, or fall to earth, it is _____ miles from its landing site.

9. As the shuttle reaches the earth's atmosphere, the surface temperature of the orbiter can reach _____ degrees Fahrenheit.

10. The tiles protecting the orbiter are called _____ tiles.

Mission Control at Johnson Space Center, Houston, Texas

Speak Out

activity 1

Do this activity in groups of three. Using only your notes on the diagrams of the mission phases and the Remote Manipulation Arm, describe the phases of the mission and the use of the RMA. Help each other out if you get stuck.

activity 2

Choose a partner for this activity. Then think of a city or town that you are very familiar with and enjoy. Give your partner a "minitour" of this city or town while he or she takes notes and asks questions. Here are some kinds of information you might want to include in your tour:

- points of historical interest
- shopping areas
- museums
- city or town hall
- tourist attractions, such as amusement parks, zoos, theaters
- schools and universities
- geographical attractions (lakes, rivers, mountains)
- transportation systems

After describing and discussing the town and asking and answering questions about it, class members should be able to make a two- or three-minute report on their partner's chosen city. If you prefer, you may take your partner on a minitour of someplace other than a town—for example, a college, a factory, or a resort that you know well.

SKILL B

Shifting Focus

Using the Passive Voice

As you heard in the previous simulation, instructors tend to use an impersonal, rather formal English. To create a feeling of objectivity, they often use the passive voice. Here are some hints to help you recognize the passive voice and to help you compare it with the active voice.

- A verb in the passive voice consists of a form of the verb to be plus a past participle.
  example: The shuttle was flown.

- Sometimes in sentences using the passive voice, the "doer" of the action is mentioned, but the "doer" is not as important as the subject of the sentence.

  example: The shuttle was flown by a pilot.

  Notice the use of the word "by" and the impersonal tone of the sentence.

- In contrast, in active voice sentences the "doer" is the subject of the sentence and the focus of attention.

  example: My aunt flew the shuttle.

  Notice that the sentence contains a personal reference. It is does not have the same neutral, impersonal tone of a passive voice sentence. In fact, the speaker could even be bragging a little.

Conversations

In the following four conversations, you will hear the active voice contrasted with the passive voice, and the personal with the impersonal. Listen to the conversations and answer the questions after conversations 2 and 4.

conversation 1 A mother and father are standing in the front yard talking.

conversation 2 Two policemen are talking to each other.

1. Which conversation (1 or 2) contains the passive voice?

   _____

   _____

2. Why do you think the passive voice was used in this situation?

   _____

   _____

conversation 3 A husband and wife are in the living room talking.

conversation 4 A woman is on the phone with an electric company employee.

1. Which conversation (3 or 4) contains the passive voice?

   _____

   _____

2. Why do you think the passive voice was used in this situation?

   _____

   _____

Listen In

Look at the following incomplete sentences. Read them to yourself and then be prepared to listen for the complete sentences as you hear the lecture for the third time. The sentences are all in the passive voice and appear in the order of their occurrence in the lecture. Complete the sentences with the correct forms of the verbs in parentheses.

1. "At T minus zero the booster rockets on either side fire, and three seconds later we _____ (lift) off the ground by the combined energy of the five engines."

2. "Two minutes after takeoff the fuel in the booster rockets _____ (use up)."

3. "Since the failure of its control system, the satellite has been going through space without guidance—going so fast that it cannot _____ (reach) directly by the Remote Manipulation Arm."

4. "The 'hand,' or what _____ (call) the end effector, _____ (fit) with three inside wires."

5. "A short arm of the satellite _____ (catch) by these wires."

6. "Remember, we said that the satellite was moving too quickly _____ (pick up) directly by the RMA."

7. "We hear Mission Control Houston through the wall speakers: 'Your mission _____ (accomplish)!'"

8. "We _____ (protect) by thermal tiles covering the ship from surface temperatures of 2750 degrees Fahrenheit."

9. "The heat is so great that radio communications _____ (block) for twelve minutes of our descent."

Speak Out

Step 1   Coastal areas and deserts are often chosen as sites for space centers and bases. With a partner, try to think of at least two reasons for this. Then give your suggestions for playing the following roles.

- One partner is the head of Space Administration. You are talking by telephone to the person in charge of selecting the next site for a U.S. space base. Tell him or her where to build the base and why. Use the active voice; you are directly involved.
- The other partner is a professor telling a classroom of students about the placement of space bases in the United States. Tell them where they are located and why. Use the passive voice; you are not directly involved.

Step 2 Present your role-play to the class. Discuss the relationship of passive and active voice to the characterizations.

activity **2**

Radio and TV announcers try to remain impersonal and detached from the stories they report; the passive voice is often used in news reporting. Here are some "facts" about an imaginary accident at a U.S. space base. As a class or in small groups, take turns adding a sentence to the report, using the passive voice and the cues provided. Note that the events are in chronological order and in the past. The first one is done as an example. You may add additional items if you wish.

Yesterday there was a tragic fire after a lift-off on launch pad number 2.

1. the astronauts / give

The astronauts were given their breakfast at 5:00 A.M.

2. the countdown / begin

3. the astronauts / ask

4. the controls / check

5. all systems / test

6. the signal / give

Suddenly a fire broke out in the booster rockets before the spaceship took off.

7. the astronauts' cabin / fill

8. the fire / put out

9. the pilots / kill

10. two mechanics / injure

11. Mission Control / shock

12. burned pieces / find

13. the public / inform

14. the next mission / cancel

activity 3

Consider an event that you or someone else in the class experienced or witnessed (or you may listen to a radio or TV news report and take notes). Then report this event to the class in the style of a news report. You may make this report humorous or serious, as you wish. Use the passive voice to create an impersonal tone.

Technicians and officials at Cape Canaveral, Florida, inspect a spacecraft in which three astronauts lost their lives in a flash fire on the launching pad.

focus on testing

You will hear two speakers. After each speaker finishes talking, you will hear a question. To answer the question, read the four possible answers and decide which one is the best answer. Circle the letter of the best answer.

SPEAKER 1

A. A plane has crashed.
B. Bad weather has closed down the airport.
C. The pilots have refused to fly the planes.
D. A bomb has been dropped on the airport.

SPEAKER 2

A. Why the space shuttle will not take off today.
B. When the repairs for the shuttle are scheduled to happen.
C. Why the airport bus will not be running.
D. What kind of repairs are needed.

CHAPTER SIX

Money Matters

You will listen to a radio program called "The World Bank Under Fire." It describes how the World Bank is trying to help developing nations and explores some problems this large financial institution is having.

Skill A—Learning Strategy: Listening for Pros and Cons
(Arguments For and Against)

Skill B—Language Function: Agreeing and Disagreeing

- **In 1993 the World Bank loaned more than $18 billion to nations needing assistance with economic development. At that point, the bank held $140 billion in loans to developing nations.**

- **Most of the money loaned by the World Bank is used for electric power, transportation, and communication projects.**

- **Some people disagree with some of the projects the World Bank helps support. They question the value of building a dam to provide water for crops when it makes thousands of people homeless and destroys forests along with endangered plants and animals.**

Getting Started
Sharing Your Experience

activity

Whether banks are friends or enemies depends on one's point of view. As a class, or in small groups, discuss the following questions.

1. Think of a person or family you know who has been helped or hurt by a bank. What did the bank do? How did this affect the people involved?
2. What business do you know about that depends on a bank for its operation? What does the bank do for the business? Try to describe ways that the bank has helped and hurt this company.

Banks are often seen as friends in time of need. For instance, when the owner of a small business wants to expand, the local banker may be the first person to see. Or, when a busy salesperson has to replace a car, she or he often rushes to the loan department of the nearest bank.

On the other hand, some people think that banks are their worst enemies. One example might be the struggling young family that finds it impossible to pay the mortgage on their home because of illness or unemployment. The bank forecloses and can then take away the property.

Vocabulary

The following vocabulary items are some words in the radio program on the World Bank that may be new to you.

to alleviate	*to lessen or make easier*
to borrow	*to take something with permission (with the intention of returning it)*
breeding	*sexual reproduction of animals*
environmental	*relating to the living conditions experienced by plants, animals, and people*
insiders	*people in a group or organization who have special knowledge of its workings*
to invest	*to put money into a project in order to earn more money*
irrigation	*watering of farmland by canals, ditches, and so on*
to loan	*to give something (with the intention of getting it back)*
proposal	*suggestion*
snail	*a simple animal in a coiled shell*
under fire	*under attack; needing defense*

exercise Use the correct forms of the vocabulary words to complete this crossword puzzle. (Answers are on page 76.)

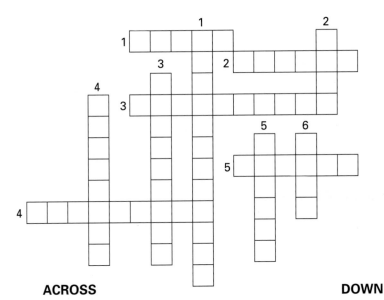

ACROSS

1. Rabbits and mice do this rapidly.
2. What you do when you need money.
3. Dry lands need this in order to produce food.
4. Sometimes money can . . . the problems of the poor.
5. Few people eat them.

DOWN

1. Air and water pollution problems are . . . problems.
2. You hope that the bank will . . . you money.
3. What businesspeople often study before making decisions.
4. These people are "in the know."
5. A banker will tell you how to . . . your money.
6. She really defended her position well when she was under . . .

SKILL A

Listening for Pros and Cons (Arguments For and Against)

Speakers often state arguments for and against the points they are making. These arguments are called pros and cons. In order to call attention to both the pro and the con arguments, a speaker uses words that indicate a switch from one point of view to the other. For example, if your investment banker suggests that it is a good idea to invest in a certain company, she or he will probably also tell you that there are certain risks involved:

> Now is definitely the time to buy into this company. It's just beginning to grow and it's not well known yet, so you can buy shares at a very good price. However, there's always the chance that the company will grow too quickly and not be able to manage this growth well. In that case, you could lose some money here.

After telling why it's a good idea to invest in the company (giving a pro argument), the speaker uses the word however to introduce some negative information (a "con" argument).

Words and Expressions Used to Change Your Point of View

although	nonetheless
but	on the contrary
however	on the other hand
instead	

Listen In

You are going to listen to a radio program called "The World Bank Under Fire." The program is hosted by Michelle Barney, the radio station's financial reporter. She interviews a special guest from the World Bank and asks the guest some very challenging questions. Listen for the pros and cons concerning three World Bank Agencies.

Step 1 First listen to the program once all the way through.

Step 2 Then listen to the program again and fill in the chart on the facing page as you listen. Be sure to look at the chart carefully before you begin. You may need to listen to the program several times in order to fill in the chart completely.

Water pump for irrigation of field crops in Egypt, a World Bank project

World Bank President Lewis Preston addresses the annual meeting, 1994

Member Agencies for the World Bank

International Bank for Reconstruction and Development	International Development Association (IDA)	International Finance Corporation (IFC)
Pros (Advantages)	*Pros (Advantages)*	*Pros (Advantages)*
1. _____ _____	1. _____ _____	1. _____ _____
2. _____ _____	2. _____ _____	2. _____ _____
Cons (Disadvantages)	*Cons (Disadvantages)*	*Cons (Disadvantages)*
1. _____ _____	1. _____ _____	1. _____ _____
2. _____ _____	2. _____ _____	2. _____ _____

Speak Out

Deciding the best way to spend and invest money is a problem not only for ministers of finance but for the "little guy" as well. The average person tries to save some money every month, and over time these savings build up. The question at that point is what to do with the money. Do you stuff it in a mattress for a rainy day (most experts would cry at the thought!), or do you attempt to put your money to work for you so that the amount grows? Here are some possible ways to invest money.

- Buy a condominium. Rent it now and sell it later at a profit.
- Buy individual stocks on the stock market.
- Buy mutual funds.
- Place your money into a bank account that pays above-average interest.
- Buy 1,000 lottery tickets.

$ $ $ $
Guaranteed Rates
for the
Serious Investor

INVESTMENT CERTIFICATES

$10,000 "Mini Jumbo"

TERM	RATE	YIELD
3 MONTHS	3.25	3.29
6 MONTHS	3.60	3.67
12 MONTHS	3.92	4.00

$100,000 "Giant Jumbo"

TERM	RATE	YIELD
3 MONTHS	3.35	3.39
6 MONTHS	3.60	3.67
12 MONTHS	3.95	4.03

$10,00 minimum investment on "Mini Jumbo" and $100,000 minimum investment on "Giant Jumbo.' Penalty for early withdrawal. Available to California residents only.
Interest paid monthly or deposited to passbook account.

(LIMITED OFFER)

FIRESIDE *Thrift*

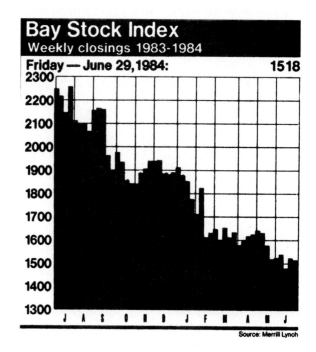

Bay Stock Index
Weekly closings 1983-1984
Friday — June 29,1984: 1518

Source: Merrill Lynch

activity

Of course, there are many pros and cons involved in each type of investment. For this activity, imagine you have saved $25,000.

Step 1 Divide into small groups to discuss the pros and cons of these investments. Each group should try to list as many pros and cons as they can think of for each type of investment.

Step 2 Examine your group's list of pros and cons carefully. Then take a vote on which investment your group thinks is the best.

Step 3 Report the results of the voting to the rest of the class.

Step 4 At this point you might want to suggest additional investment options. List all the suggestions on the board. Discuss the pros and cons of each suggestion.

Agreeing and Disagreeing

When instructors give a point of view, they expect students to be able to react to their statements by agreeing or disagreeing. They admire students who are able to express their own points of view. This is considered independent thinking and is valued. Of course, being able to agree or disagree is valuable outside as well as inside the classroom. All of us are called upon daily to give our points of view in conversations with friends, relatives, and acquaintances.

To feel comfortable when we make a point, we need to know the vocabulary of agreeing and disagreeing. We also need to know which expressions are polite and which are not.

Expressions for Expressing Agreement

INFORMAL	FORMAL
Exactly.	I agree.
I'll say!	I agree with that.
I knew it!	I couldn't agree more.
Okay!	Exactly. (Exactly right.)
That's right.	That's absolutely true.
That's for sure!	That's correct.
You'd better believe it!	That's precisely the point.
You can say that again!	

Conversations

Listen to the following conversations in which expressions of agreement and disagreement are used both correctly and incorrectly.

conversation 1 In a college classroom, a student is challenging an instructor. Listen to the speakers and answer the questions.

Do you think the student is being polite or rude? _____

Why? _____

conversation 2 Now listen to another student respond to the same instructor and answer the questions.

Do you think this student responded appropriately? _____

Why? _____

conversation 3 Two students are chatting in the school cafeteria. Listen to the speakers and answer the question.

Paul probably doesn't have too many friends. Why do you think this might be?

_____

conversation 4 Let's give Paul another chance to respond to Roger a bit more appropriately. Listen, and then answer the question.

Why is the expression that Paul uses this time to agree with Roger much more appropriate? _____

conversation 5 At a corporation meeting, two board members are discussing future plans. Listen to the speakers and answer the questions.

Do you think these board members will reach consensus easily? _____

Why or why not? _____

conversation 6 Now listen to two other board members in a similar conversation. Answer the questions.

1. Do you think these board members will be able to reach an agreement more or less easily than the board members in the previous conversation? _____

2. How is this conversation different from the previous one? _____

_____

conversation 7 At the doctor's office, a doctor and her patient's wife are discussing the patient. Listen to the speakers and answer the questions.

1. Is Mrs. Franklin, the patient's wife, agreeing or disagreeing with the doctor? _____

2. Is Mrs. Franklin responding formally or informally? _____

conversation 8 Listen to the doctor and Mrs. Franklin again. This time Mrs. Franklin responds differently. Answer the questions.

1. Is Mrs. Franklin responding formally or informally? _____

2. Which of the two responses do you think is more appropriate and why?

_____

Listen In

exercise 1

You are going to listen to the program again. This time your instructor will stop the tape eight times so that you can have the opportunity to agree or disagree with the speaker. Before listening to the tape, go over the following sentences. They will be the last sentences you hear before your instructor stops the tape, so it is important that you understand them thoroughly.

Stop 1   *"But it turns out that money isn't everything."*

Stop 2   *". . . irrigation projects to raise farm production won't make more money for a country if the government of that country keeps food prices too low."*

Stop 3   *"Well, this is good for the countries that want to sell goods to developing countries, but wouldn't this discourage local production of goods?"*

Stop 4   *". . . we know that technological advances can sometimes cause environmental problems . . ."*

Stop 5   *". . . an understanding of the local culture and needs may be more important than anything else for the success of a project."*

Stop 6   *"This is good for the country because the government does not have to guarantee the loan and it encourages the growth of private business or industry."*

Stop 7   *". . . the best loans have no strings attached, right?"*

Stop 8   *". . . we all know that it is difficult to separate economic goals and political interests in today's world."*

exercise 2

Now listen to the program again. Have the list of expressions from the Skill B section in front of you so that you can practice expressing your points of view politely and formally.

- When you agree with a point, support your idea with an example from your own experience.
- When you disagree, give your reason.

Speak Out

activity 1

Step 1   As a whole class, go over the following information about the nearly bankrupt country of Almost Broke.

Step 2   Divide into two groups. Each group should come up with at least five actions that could be taken to improve the economic conditions in Almost Broke.

Step 3   Take turns reporting your group's suggestions or proposals for action.

- When a suggestion is made by the other group, the members of your group should say whether they agree or disagree with the proposal and why.

- Practice using the expressions of agreement and disagreement presented in this chapter. Begin with formal expressions, then, as the discussion continues, use the stronger, less polite expressions if you wish.

THE LAND OF ALMOST BROKE

abundant natural resources (recently discovered): oil, uranium
a common language (spoken by all)
several large towns
several large rivers flowing from the mountains
a large lake
a pleasant climate
a mountainous central region

landlocked (no outlet to the sea)

only one major export
imports greatly exceed exports
high unemployment rate
high illiteracy rate
high inflation rate
poor soil
a large population
a low hourly wage
unfriendly neighbors

Step 1   Locate a newspaper or magazine article that you feel strongly about and bring a copy to class.

Step 2   Summarize the major issue in the article for the class.

Step 3   State the author's point of view and explain why you agree or disagree. Use the stronger, less polite forms of disagreement. However, be aware that the expressions you use often say more about you than about the topic you are discussing.

You will hear two speakers. After each speaker finishes talking, you will hear a question. To answer the question, read the four possible answers and decide which one is the best answer. Circle the letter of the best answer.

SPEAKER 1

A. Banks are loaning less money to poor people than in the past.
B. There are pros and cons in accepting bank loans.
C. The bank gives away money to the poor.
D. Banks use string to tie up sacks of money.

SPEAKER 2

A. I didn't understand what you said.
B. I don't agree with you.
C. It can take years to save enough money to buy something.
D. You will save money if you pay cash for something.

Answer to puzzle on page 67:

		1				2	
1 B	R	E	E	D		L	
	3	N	2 B	O	R	R	O W
4	P	V				A	
I	3 I	R	R	I	G A T I O N		
N	O	R	5	6			
S	P	O	I	F			
I	O	N	5 S	N A	I L S		
D	S	M	V	R			
4 A L L E	V I A T E	N	E	E			
R	L	T	S				
S	S	A	T				
		L					

CHAPTER seven

Leisure Time

in this chapter

You will listen to a public lecture called "Leisure Time in Our Society."
The lecture is followed by a question and answer session.

Skill A—Learning Strategy: Listening for Chronological Order

Skill B—Language Function: Expressing Likes and Dislikes

DID YOU KNOW?

- **At one time in China, people who didn't have to work received the highest degree of respect. It was the custom for Chinese noblemen to let their fingernails grow very long to show that they were not required to work.**

- **The average American man or woman now works 163 hours per year more than in 1969. Americans now spend nearly 2,000 hours per year on the job. And this is in addition to 900 hours per year of work around the house.**

- **In Sweden, the law requires that companies give their employees 5 weeks of vacation per year. In Belgium, it's 4 weeks. Most workers in the United States start out with 2 weeks per year.**

Getting Started
Sharing Your Experience

In today's technological society, holidays tend to commemorate political rather than religious events. Of the main holidays in the United States for which employees get a day off work, only two are religious in nature.

MEMO

To: All employees

From: D.J. Paterson, President, Paterson Electronics

Re: Company holidays

F.Y.I.

This year we will observe the following holidays:

New Year's Day

Martin Luther King Day

President's Day

Good Friday (we will close at 2 p.m.)

Memorial Day

Fourth of July

Labor Day

Thanksgiving (Thursday and Friday)

Christmas Eve (we will close at 2 p.m.)

Christmas Day

One personal leave day of your choice

 In small groups, discuss the following.

1. What two U.S. holidays are religious in nature? List them.

_____

_____

2. Discuss the holidays you and your family celebrate. Are these holidays religious or nonreligious?

activity 2 As a class, make a list of the various holidays that people in the class celebrate.

HOLIDAYS	CLASSMATES WHO CELEBRATE
_____	_____
_____	_____
_____	_____
_____	_____
_____	_____
_____	_____
_____	_____

What are the two most frequently celebrated holidays and the two least frequently celebrated holidays? On which holidays are people given a paid day off from work?

Vocabulary

You will hear the following words in the lecture. Look over the words and their definitions and use the following exercises to help you remember them.

aggressively	*forcefully, energetically*
counterpart	*equivalent, similar type*
distinction	*difference*
to evolve	*to develop over a long period of time*
notion	*idea*
perspective	*view, viewpoint*
to pursue	*to follow, chase*
saint	*holy or godly person*
textile	*cloth*
trend	*tendency*

 **exercise 1**   Match the following words without looking back at the definitions.

1. _____ to pursue
2. _____ counterpart
3. _____ notion
4. _____ saint
5. _____ trend
6. _____ to evolve
7. _____ distinction
8. _____ aggressive
9. _____ textile

a. to develop slowly
b. idea
c. forceful
d. tendency
e. difference
f. holy person
g. cloth
h. equivalent
i. to chase

 **exercise 2**   In small groups, return to your discussion of holidays and days off from work. Take turns saying a sentence or two on the topic. Try to use at least one of the vocabulary words during each turn.

SKILL A

Listening for Chronological Order

Chronological order is a method of organization based on time. Simple chronological order takes the reader or listener from a point in the past to a point closer to the present (or to the present itself). History is often presented in simple chronological order.

Most lectures, however, are more complex than just a presentation of facts or ideas in chronological order. The lecture in this chapter is a good example of the way chronological order serves as the foundation for a complex presentation of facts. In order to compare present-day ideas of leisure with those of the past, the speaker moves forward and backward in time.

Note the following expressions that indicate time or sequence. They will help you follow the speaker's train of thought.

Time and Sequence Words

after	long ago
afterward	next
before	now
by . . . (time)	past
during	present
eventually	present day
finally	presently
first	recently
formerly	soon
from . . . to . . .	then
in . . . (date)	today
in . . . (adjective) times	until
last	while
later	

Listen In

Look at the chart and statements on page 82 before you listen to the lecture. When you are sure that you understand the chart, start to listen. As you listen, decide the time frame for each statement on the chart and indicate it with an X. In one case you will need to mark more than one time period for a statement. The first one has been done for you.

statements	prehistoric times	4th century: Roman times	13th century: medieval times	1700s–1800s: Industrial Age	1900s: present times
1. Workers begin to punch time clocks.				X	
2. Workers see no distinction between work and play.					
3. Workers pursue leisure time aggressively.					
4. The 2,000-hour work year is common.					
5. The work week of the common worker begins to increase.					
6. Workers are relatively affluent.					
7. The term *worker* includes many categories.					
8. The word *worker* referred to clerical workers and skilled craftsmen and excluded common laborers and women.					
9. Holidays are more likely to be named after presidents than saints.					
10. Labor unions argue that a worker's birthday should be considered a holiday for that worker.					

Mosaic One • Listening/Speaking

Speak Out

In order to keep track of the time sequence of the incidents mentioned in a lecture, you must listen for time and sequence words that indicate chronological order. It is also important to follow the logic of the facts being presented. Use the following as clues to understanding chronological order:

- common sense
- word repetition
- the use of pronouns to refer to previously mentioned nouns
- the choice of definite and indefinite articles (*the* vs. *a*)

activity **1**

Work in small groups. Read the three sentences aloud. Then use the clues above to help you answer the questions.

1. The bus came but her friend didn't get off.
2. Marcia was waiting for a friend to arrive by bus.
3. Eventually, Marcia called her friend to find out what had happened.

Which of the sentences would come first? _____

Why? _____

Which would come second? _____

Why? _____

Which is third? _____

Why? _____

activity **2**

Work in groups of five or six. Use the story starter below as a the first line of a story. The first student reads the sentence and continues the story by adding another sentence. Continue in this manner until every student has had two turns. Look at the list of time and sequence words on page 81 and use as many of them as you can as you tell the story.

> *Story Starter:* Since this was the first day off that Jane had had in over a week, she intended to put her feet up and enjoy a good book. But that isn't what happened!

activity **3**

Do another story activity with the whole class. Make up a new story starter and take turns adding sentences to it. If possible, stay with the topic of leisure-time activities.

SKILL B

Expressing Likes and Dislikes

Everyone has likes and dislikes, and you will frequently find yourself in situations in which you have the chance to express them. A variety of expressions can be used for this purpose. The nature of the situation (whether it's formal or informal, for example) must be considered before choosing which expression to use.

Of course, even in very informal situations the feelings of others must be considered. If you are going to make a statement indicating dislike, you might want to use an expression that would soften it—make it less strong. When choosing between making a gentle or a strong statement, you should also consider your tone of voice. Tone of voice is often more important than the actual expression you choose.

The following expressions are some of the most common ones used for expressing likes and dislikes. They are listed in order from the gentlest to the strongest. In situations in which it is best not to be outspoken, the strongest statements are not appropriate.

	Expressions for Expressing Likes	**Expressions for Expressing Dislikes**
least strong	I like . . .	I don't especially like . . .
	I enjoy . . .	I don't care for . . .
	I'm pleased by . . .	I dislike . . .
	I'm happy to . . .	I don't have time for . . .
	I appreciate . . .	I can't tolerate . . .
	I'm delighted by . . .	. . . irks me/bugs me. (informal)
	This is my idea of . . .	. . . is more than I can stand.
	I'm tickled by . . .	I can't take/stand/bear . . .
	That's terrific/great/super!	What a rotten . . .
	What a terrific/great/super . . . !	I abhor . . .
strongest	I love . . .	I hate . . .

Conversations

Listen to the taped conversations. They demonstrate a wide variety of ways to express likes and dislikes.

conversation 1 A man is being interviewed for a job. Listen to the speakers and answer the questions.

Do you think the man will get the job? _____

Why or why not? _____

_____

A woman is being interviewed for a job. Listen to the speakers and answer the questions.

Do you think the woman will get the job? _____

Why or why not? _____

_____

conversation 3

Rafael and Ana are discussing what to do with their leisure time. Listen to the speakers and answer the questions.

1. Does Ana enjoy rock concerts? _____

2. Does she express her opinion strongly, or does she soften it? _____

_____

3. Do you think Rafael will ask Ana out again? _____

Why or why not? _____

_____

conversation 4

Rafael and Joyce are discussing what to do with their leisure time. Listen to the speakers and answer the questions.

1. Does Joyce enjoy experimental theater? _____

2. Does she express her opinion strongly? _____

3. Do you think Rafael will ask Joyce out again? _____

Why or why not? _____

_____

Listen In

At several points in the lecture on leisure time, the speaker expresses a like or a dislike. The speaker also asks the audience a few things about their likes and dislikes.

exercise

Listen to the lecture again. This time, in the space provided, jot down all the lecturer's likes and dislikes that you can. Later, compare your notes with those of your classmates.

_____

_____

_____

_____

_____

Speak Out

activity

Listen to the lecture again. When the lecturer asks a question about your likes or dislikes, stop the tape and answer it before listening to more of the lecture. Practice using the expressions on page 84 to express your likes and dislikes in response to these questions.

activity 2

Look over the following chart of leisure-time activities. Circle those things that you really enjoy, and make an X through the ones you do not like very much. Add other likes and dislikes in the blank boxes. As a class or in smaller groups, discuss why you marked your charts the way you did. Use expressions on page 84 as necessary to express your likes and dislikes.

Most Americans have 2 weeks of paid vacation a year.

Do You Like or Dislike . . . ?

art	sports	food	music	television	dancing	reading	other
art museums	jogging	Japanese	rock 'n' roll	old movies	rock 'n' roll	newspapers	
photo exhibits	tennis	Mexican	classical	soap operas	ballet	novels	
international crafts	weight lifting	Italian	jazz	news	tap	magazines	
natural history museums	skiing	American	rap	cartoons	toe	short stories	
painting	bicycle riding	Indian	soul	documentaries	jazz	textbooks	
ceramics	judo	Chinese	country and western	weekly comedy series	modern	poetry	

activity **3**

Do this activity in groups of five or six. For each of the situations below, decide what to say to the person you encounter and to the friend who is with you. Choose an appropriate expression and tone of voice for each exchange. Share your responses with other members of the group. The first one is done as an example.

1. A man sitting in front of you at the movie theater has three noisy children with him. They are throwing popcorn at each other and talking too much. You have already asked the father politely to do something about the situation, but there has been no change. It's time to take stronger action.

   To the father: I would really appreciate it if you would quiet down your children.

   To your friend: Let's move; I can't stand this.

2. You are a single woman out with your friends at a club. You are enjoying yourself with your friends and do not want to be bothered by anyone. However, a man keeps asking you if you want to dance, and you have already refused him twice. You see now that he is coming over to your table again.

   To the man: _____

   To your friends: _____

3. For several years you have been eating at a local restaurant. The food has been good, the atmosphere pleasant, and the service friendly and attentive. Lately, however, things have changed. The new waiters don't seem to care about you, the restaurant doesn't seem as clean as before, and the food is often mediocre. You and a friend have decided to give the restaurant one last chance, and as you are eating a tasteless stew, the owner approaches you and asks you if everything is all right.

   To the owner: _____

   To your friend: _____

4. You and a friend have enrolled in a real estate class. Unfortunately, the instructor often digresses from the subject, telling long and uninteresting stories about his travels. You want to spend your time learning more about real estate.

   To the instructor: _____

   To your friend: _____

5. You and a colleague have become involved in a charity fund-raising campaign at work. You have enjoyed helping out with the bookkeeping, but now your supervisor has requested that you ask your colleagues directly for contributions. You have already said that you are not comfortable doing this, but the supervisor has continued to insist that you help in this way.

   To the supervisor: _____

   To your friend: _____

You will hear two speakers. After each speaker finishes talking, you will hear a question. To answer the question, read the four possible answers and decide which one is the best answer. Circle the letter of the best answer.

SPEAKER 1

A. Garage sales are a waste of time.
B. Looking at other people is ridiculous.
C. Sunday is the best day of the week.
D. Sunday is a good day for a garage sale.

SPEAKER 2

A. Chocolate is lucky.
B. A dinner of only chocolate desserts is a good idea.
C. Every dinner should have a chocolate dessert.
D. All pot luck dinners include chocolate desserts.

CHAPTER eight
Creativity

You will listen to a lecture and class discussion in an introductory engineering class. The title of the lecture is "Creativity: As Essential to the Engineer as to the Artist."

Skill A—Learning Strategy: Listening for Signal Words

Skill B—Language Function: Divulging Information

- Grandma Moses (Anna Mary Robertson Moses) lived on a farm all her life and never had a single art lesson. However, when she was over 70 she began to paint and went on to become a widely known and very successful artist.

- Wolfgang Amadeus Mozart was regarded as a creative genius by the time he was 5 years old. His ability to compose and perform music was far beyond that of most well-trained adult musicians of his time.

- R. Buckminster Fuller was a revolutionary architect and inventor who came up with ways of getting the most use out of the least amount of material. He is best known for the "geodesic dome," an inexpensive style of building that can be used for homes, workshops, barns, or storage.

R. Buckminster Fuller in front of a geodesic dome

Getting Started
Sharing Your Experience

Being creative is not limited to scientists or artists. There is a multitude of amateur inventors who keep finding new and more convenient ways of doing everyday things. For example, the paper clip was invented by a man who kept losing his paperwork. In addition to becoming a millionaire, he became very well organized!

A unique invention for commuting

activity 1

In small groups, discuss the following list of inventions and describe how they are creative solutions to everyday problems. In your discussion, you might consider the things they replaced.

- typewriter
- adding machine
- lightbulb
- washing machine

- ballpoint pen
- refrigerator
- rubber band

activity 2

Often we are unable to see the potential uses for familiar objects. In small groups, closely look at an ordinary object such as a rubber band, a ballpoint pen, or a safety pin for a brief time. Make a list of ten things you could do with the object (aside from its normal use, of course). Share your findings with the group.

activity 3

Here's another group activity to stimulate new thoughts. Sit in a circle if possible. Take any ordinary object you see around you: a cup, a leaf, a pencil, a sweater. Give the object you have to the person on your left, and take the object from the person on your right. Now, let your thoughts flow as freely as you can about how the object you are now holding represents your personality (or the personality of someone you know or someone famous, living or dead). Try to think of at least five examples and share these with the group. For instance:

A LEAF . . .

- can be very fragile and so am I at times.
- can be very strong and durable and so am I at times.
- goes through many changes in its lifetime and so do I.
- is flexible and bends easily and most of the time I do too.
- just hangs around and I like to do that too.

Vocabulary

The following words from the lecture relate to key aspects of the topic of creativity. Learn the words by studying their meanings and filling in the blanks in the following sentences.

analytical	*referring to close examination of something*
to circumnavigate	*to go completely around something*
fragmentary	*broken into parts*
to fuse	*to bind together*
to inhibit	*to block or frustrate*
original	*unique, the first one of its kind*
solution	*answer to a problem*
to specialize	*to limit to a very narrow area of use or study*

 Fill in the blanks with the appropriate form of the vocabulary word.

1. If you have a very _____ mind, you will tend to examine both objects and issues very closely.

2. Ferdinand Magellan was the first man to _____ the earth.

3. Emotions will often _____ clear thinking.

4. Intense heat may _____ the nuclei of two atoms.

5. He couldn't find a _____ to the problem because his knowledge of the subject was incomplete and

_____ .

6. If you _____ too much in any field of knowledge, you will tend to lose sight of its relation to other aspects of life.

7. To develop your own identity, you can't always imitate others; you have to

be _____ .

SKILL A

Listening for Signal Words

In speaking and writing, we often use signal words to prepare our audience for what is to come, what our next idea will be. This allows the audience to listen more effectively. Listening for signal words is especially important when attending a lecture because it aids us in taking notes. If an instructor says, "Now I'm going to outline today's subject for you," we know to prepare ourselves to do outlining. If the instructor says, "Now I'm going to review yesterday's material," we know to think about the topic covered the day before and perhaps to look back over our previous notes. Signal words prepare us for what is going to happen next and what we need to do in response.

Verbs That Serve as Signal Words		
analyze	emphasize	outline
answer	evaluate	pick up (where we left off)
consider	explain	reiterate
continue	go on (with)	repeat
criticize	go over	review
define	illustrate	summarize
describe	justify	
discuss	list	

Listen In

To practice listening for signal words used in the lecture, follow these instructions.

Step 1 Listen to the lecture once all the way through to get the main idea.

Step 2 Listen again, keeping in mind the signal words on the list. Every time you hear one of these words or phrases, write it in the space provided on page 94. Listen until you have found at least six signal words.

Step 3 Listen to the lecture a third time. This time pay particular attention to what happens after each signal word or phrase. Note in the spaces provided what the speaker does after each signal word. (*Hint:* If the lecturer has used the signal word effectively, your answer will include a definition or synonym for this word.) The first two are done as examples.

Georges Seurat used dots of color to create his painting
Afternoon on the Island of La Grande Jatte.

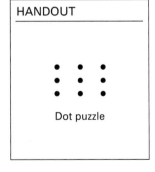

HANDOUT

Dot puzzle

SIGNAL WORD(S)	WHAT COMES NEXT; WHAT THE LECTURER DOES
1. continue	goes on with the discussion of the creative process
2. pick up where we left off	begins with the idea started at the end of the last class
_____	_____
_____	_____
_____	_____
_____	_____
_____	_____
_____	_____
_____	_____
_____	_____
_____	_____
_____	_____
_____	_____
_____	_____
_____	_____
_____	_____

Speak Out

activity **1**

We have been discussing the way signaling occurs in language. But other kinds of signaling go on all the time among human beings, animals, insects, plants, and even individual units of life called cells. For example, cells send chemical messages to one another; plants use pollen, scent, and insects to send messages; birds use markings—or the color of their feathers—and sound.

Below are the names of some animals and insects that are well known for their ability to signal and communicate:

whales	ants	monkeys	mockingbirds
bees	dogs	porpoises	cockroaches

Step 1 Form small discussion groups. Each person should choose one of the animals or insects listed (or another you may know about).

Step 2 Do some research to find out how it signals and communicates.

Step 3   Meet with your groups again. Take turns describing the major ways each animal or insect communicates.

Step 4   Discuss these questions:

- How do these animal forms of communication compare to human communication?
- Are they as creative?

activity **2**

In small groups, share solutions to the following thought problem: If you were placed in a cell with another person and not allowed to speak or write, what methods would you devise to communicate with the other person?

activity **3**

Human beings use more than language to signal each other. Two nonverbal signals that people use every day—often unconsciously—are tone of voice and body language. Tone of voice and body language tell us how people really feel despite their words. As people's moods change, their voices and bodies reflect those changes. If you are alert, you can read the deeper meanings of the words people say by noticing the tone in which they speak and their posture, gestures, and other body language while they speak.

Step 1   To get a feeling for nonverbal communication, push back the desks (if possible) and form a large circle with your classmates and instructor.

Step 2   Take turns saying an insignificant sentence to someone across the room from you. Your instructor or a classmate will suggest an adjective to describe your attitude as you say the sentence.

Step 3   When it is your turn, take a few steps as you say the sentence to get your whole body into the act, not just your face and voice. Here's a sentence you can use, or you can make up your own if you prefer.

Apples are red and bananas are yellow.

Here are a few adjectives to get you started. Add as many as you can to this list.

angry	frightened	murderous
delighted	frustrated	rushed
disgusted	grieving	sarcastic
flirtatious	inhibited	shy

Divulging Information

To *divulge* means "to give out or disclose." In colloquial English, if someone is divulging information, the implication is that we are being told "the real stuff," "the inside information," "what is really happening."

Information that is *divulged* is of a different quality from other information given during a conversation or a lecture. It is important in note taking and outlining that you recognize when information is being divulged because it might be this information that you will be expected to take most seriously and that you will probably be tested on. When a lecturer is about to divulge something, he or she usually announces this intention.

Expressions for Divulging Information

Despite what you may believe . . .
Despite what you may have heard . . .
Here's how it really is . . .
The fact of the matter is . . .
What's really going on here is . . .

Slang Expressions for Divulging Information in Informal Situations

The deal is . . .
The real scoop is . . .
The real story is . . .
What really gives is . . .
Where it's really at is . . .

Conversations

Listen to these conversations, which present examples of ways to divulge information.

conversation 1 Albert and Bonnie are discussing the real reason that Professor Finster was fired. Listen to the speakers and answer the questions.

1. Is this conversation formal or informal?_____

2. What phrase helped you decide this?_____

_____

 **conversation 2** Kate and Doug are discussing where Jules got the money for his new motorcycle. Listen to the speakers and answer the questions.

1. Is this conversation formal or informal?_____

2. What phrase helped you decide this? _____

_____

Listen In

 **exercise**

Step 1 Listen to the lecture again. Pick out the phrases that signal that information is about to be divulged. Write them down in the spaces provided.

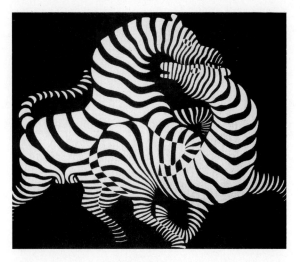

Victor Vasarely inventively used curved lines and bars of black and white to create *Zebras*.

PHRASES THE LECTURER USES WHEN DIVULGING INFORMATION

1. _____

2. _____

3. _____

4. _____

5. _____

Step 2 Now listen to the lecture again. Is the information that the lecturer divulges in this way critical to the main points of the lecture?

Why or why not?_____

_____

Discuss your responses with your classmates.

Chapter Eight • Creativity **97**

Speak Out

Step 1 Look at the following incomplete conversations. Only the first line or two of dialogue is provided for you. Choose a partner and together complete as many of the conversations as you can in the time you are given. Use as many of the expressions for divulging information as you can.

Step 2 Then select the conversation that you and your partner enjoyed doing the most and present it to the rest of the class. You might want to take notes on the lines provided.

1. A: What's up? I hear Frank's moving to Toledo.

   B: Nah, _____

   _____

   A: _____

   _____

   B: _____

   _____

2. A: I don't understand this at all. Helen tells me one thing and Jean tells me another. What's going on?

   B: _____

   _____

   A: _____

   _____

   B: _____

   _____

3. A: I just saw Alan and he looked pretty upset. What's the story? He said he was just a little tired, but he looked really worried to me.

   B: _____

   _____

   A: _____

   _____

   B: _____

   _____

4. A: Hey, what gives? I thought you'd gotten an A in that class. Paul says that you really knocked his socks off with your last creative writing project.

B: _____

_____

A: _____

_____

B: _____

_____

5. A: Where do you think I should exhibit my paintings? Henry suggested the gallery over by the museum, but Vicki said that only tourists go there.

B: _____

_____

A: _____

_____

B: _____

_____

6. A: Hey, I thought this was supposed to be a surprise party! If we arrive at 6:00, won't he already be there? What's the scoop?

B: _____

_____

A: _____

_____

B: _____

You will hear two speakers. After each speaker finishes talking, you will hear a question. To answer the question, read the four possible answers and decide which one is the best answer. Circle the letter of the best answer.

SPEAKER 1

A. She is going to draw a picture to help the listener understand.
B. Artists should never take art lessons.
C. Creativity doesn't have to be taught.
D. There are a lot of bad paintings in art galleries.

SPEAKER 2

A. How creative you are depends on how old you are.
B. Women are more creative in some areas than men.
C. People of all sexes and ages can be creative.
D. Creativity is not an important trait for either sex to possess.

CHAPTER nine

Human Behavior

You will listen to a social psychology lecture titled "Group Dynamics." In the lecture you will learn how people behave in groups.

Skill A—Learning Strategy: Recognizing Digressions

Skill B—Language Function: Asking for Information, Seeking Confirmation, and Challenging with Tag Questions

- Americans have associations for just about every interest you can imagine. The Loyal Order of Catfish Lovers has 3,000 members, the International Laughter Society has 4,100, and there are 700,000 people in the Young American Bowling Alliance.

- An association called the Giraffe Project has 2,500 members who "stick their necks out" to help other people in ways that involve physical, financial, or social risk.

- Seven out of ten Americans belong to at least one organization that is devoted to helping others or improving the community. These people give their time without pay to improve the lives of others.

Getting Started

Sharing Your Experience

Whenever you are with other people, even one person, you are in a group. Think about where you were, what you did, and who you were with during the past twenty-four hours and complete these activities.

activity *1* Fill in the following chart.

time	were you alone?	if not alone, number of people you were with	activity
1 hour ago	_____	_____	_____
2 hours ago	_____	_____	_____
4 hours ago	_____	_____	_____
6 hours ago	_____	_____	_____
8 hours ago	_____	_____	_____
10 hours ago	_____	_____	_____
12 hours ago	_____	_____	_____
14 hours ago	_____	_____	_____
16 hours ago	_____	_____	_____
18 hours ago	_____	_____	_____
20 hours ago	_____	_____	_____
22 hours ago	_____	_____	_____
24 hours ago	_____	_____	_____

activity *2* In small groups, answer these questions.

1. How many hours were you alone? _____

2. How many hours were you with others? _____

3. What activity took up most of your time? _____

activity *3* Discuss the following questions with the whole class.

1. What types of groups did you participate in?

2. Was this a typical day for each of you? Why or why not?

3. Are people in the class similar or different in the amount of time they spend alone and in groups?

4. Would you prefer to spend more time, less time, or the same amount of time in groups? Why?

Vocabulary

The italicized words in the following sentences are used in the same manner as in the lecture in this chapter. Below each word are three definitions. Choose the definition that best fits the word as it is used in the sentence.

example: Many international students already have a particular *field* of interest.

     a. _____ a piece of land with no trees

     b. _X_ a division of academic study

     c. _____ a place where oil is found

1. Joe feels his position as president of a political group on campus is an important part of his *identity*.

     a. _____ individuality, the condition of being oneself

     b. _____ intellect, intelligence

     c. _____ innocence, lack of experience

2. A number of *random* events contributed to Joe's joining the group.

     a. _____ chance

     b. _____ classical

     c. _____ cheap

3. Joe can *pretty much* do what he wants because he shares an apartment off campus and has plenty of money.

     a. _____ never

     b. _____ hardly ever

     c. _____ almost always

4. In some cultures, *eye contact* is important when speaking to someone.

     a. _____ looking directly into someone's eyes

     b. _____ agreeing with someone

     c. _____ knowing someone's eye color

5. Before Joe can go fishing with his friends, he needs to *wind* his new line around the reel.

   a. _____ to blow

   b. _____ to plant

   c. _____ to wrap

6. Joe took five minutes at the end of a group meeting to *recap* his ideas.

   a. _____ to change

   b. _____ to bottle

   c. _____ to summarize

Recognizing Digressions

Making a Digression

Most lecturers digress from time to time. That is, they go off the topic. They do this for a number of reasons:

- A lecturer might have an interesting idea that does not relate directly to the subject but that will be interesting or amusing to the students.
- A lecturer may want to connect an abstract idea to experiences that are familiar to the students.
- A lecturer wants to help students become more involved in a particular topic. In this case the lecturer might suggest activities or readings students can do on their own.
- A lecturer sees the students getting tired and wants to give them a chance to relax for a few minutes.

> *Note:*
> - Digressions are usually used for enrichment.
> - Information in digressions is not usually included on exams.

When lecturers digress too much, students find it difficult to follow the lecture. But most lecturers are careful to point out to students when they are beginning a digression.

Sometimes a lecturer begins a digression by announcing it with an apology or request for permission. In such cases, the speaker may use one of the expressions in the box at the top of the next page.

Expressions for Announcing Digressions

If I may digress . . .
If I may stray from the subject . . .
If I may wander . . .
If you'll let me digress for a moment . . .
Let me digress . . .
Let me mention in passing that . . .
(Just) As an aside . . .
By the way . . .

Oh, I forgot to mention . . .
Oh, that makes me think of . . .
Oh, that reminds me . . .
Oh, yes . . .
To change the subject . . .
To get off the topic for a moment . . .
To go off on a tangent for a moment . . .
To wander for just a moment . . .

Returning to the Main Topic

When completing a digression, lecturers usually use certain expressions to indicate to students that they are returning to the main topic.

Expressions That Indicate a Return to the Main Topic

Anyway, as I was saying . . .
As I started to say . . .
Back to our main topic . . .
To come back to what I was saying . . .
To continue with our main point . . .
To get back to the topic at hand . . .

To go on with what I was saying . . .
To return to what I was saying . . .
Well, back to business . . .
Well, back to work . . .
Well, to continue (with the main topic) . . .

Listen In

 **exercise 1**

Read the following statements, which are taken directly from the lecture. Make an educated guess about which statements relate directly to the main points in the lecture and which statements are digressions. Mark the appropriate column to the right of the statement as you decide. The first one is done for you.

	main point	digression
1. *"This afternoon I'm going to talk to you about a topic that affects every person in this room: group dynamics."*	✓	
2. *"Today we're going to look at . . . patterns of communication in groups and then at how the group affects individual performance."*		
3. *"You all went to discussion session yesterday, didn't you?"*		

	main point	digression
4. *"It doesn't seem to matter how large the group is— only a few people talk at once."*		
5. *"Two people do over 50 percent of the talking in any group."*		
6. *"I must comment here that all the research I know about has been done in the United States and Canada."*		
7. *"The research shows that in groups of eight or more, people tend to talk to the people sitting across the table from them."*		
8. *"It seems to me that where I come from we have a social rule that doesn't make much sense."*		
9. *"If you're planning to be a matchmaker and start a romance between two of your friends, don't seat them next to each other at your next formal dinner party."*		
10. *"The research also shows that, in general, the person in the group who talks the most is regarded as the leader of the group."*		
11. *"The theory behind this type of research—research that demonstrates that people do better work in groups—is called 'social facilitation theory.'"*		
12. *"In this matter of having an audience, we're like a number of other creatures."*		
13. *"As I mentioned earlier, there is also research that demonstrates that individuals perform worse, not better, on tasks when other people are there."*		
14. *"If you can manage it, you should take tests on a stage with a group of people who are also taking the test in front of a large audience."*		
How many items did you guess were digressions?		

According to the lecturer, these racers perform better with an audience present

Step 1 Listen to the lecture one or more times. As you listen, check your guesses about the statements in Exercise 1 by noting all the phrases you hear to introduce digressions. Write them on the lines under the digressions they introduce. Also note the reasons for the digressions. Use the following abbreviations to save time:

Aud. Int. = to keep the audience interested
Con.   = to connect abstract ideas to real experiences
Add. Info. = to provide additional information
Rlx.   = to relax the audience

Step 2 Compare your findings with your classmates.

How many digressions did each person hear?_____

What was the most frequently used expression to introduce a

digression? _____

What was the most frequent reason for a digression?_____

_____

What was the least frequent reason?_____

exercise **3**   **Step 1**   Turn back to the Skill A section. Look at the expressions on page 106 that indicate a return to the main topic. Then, listen to the lecture again.

As you listen, note which expressions the lecturer uses to return to the main topic from the digressions. _____

_____

_____

_____

_____

Step 2   In small groups, compare notes and answer the following questions:

Does the lecturer sometimes return to the main topic without using one of these expressions? _____

If so, what is done instead? _____

Speak Out

   **Step 1**   Sit in on a class that interests you or attend a public lecture or meeting (for example, a meeting of the Sierra Club). Your local newspaper lists the time and place of events that are open to the public. If it is not possible for you to attend a lecture or meeting, listen to a lecture on television or radio. Public broadcasting stations frequently provide lectures on current events or interesting historical topics.

Listen for the digressions in the lecture. When you hear a digression, make a note of the phrase used to introduce it and the reason for the digression. Use the same abbreviations you used in the Listen In exercise to save time (Aud. Int., Con., Add. Info., and Rlx.). Be careful to not confuse digressions with examples!

_____

Step 2   Report your findings to your class and compare notes.

How many digressions did each person hear? _____

What is the average number of digressions per lecture class members heard? _____

What was the most frequent reason for a digression? _____

What was the least frequent reason? _____

activity 2

Since you don't usually lecture to your friends, informal conversations are often one digression after another! Actually, this applies to most informal situations—with friends, acquaintances, or relatives. As a class or in small groups, discuss the following.

1. In your culture, when would a digression be impolite? Are there any circumstances in which it would be impolite *not* to digress?

2. What are some specific reasons people might use digressions in your culture?

3. When do you think digressions are most useful?

activity 3

Step 1 Break into small groups to discuss a few of the following activities that we do in groups. Add other activities to the list if you wish.

dating
eating out
going to the movies
investing money as a group
sharing a dorm room or apartment
having a picnic
playing a team sport
studying in a group
working on a team project

Write down the topics your group has chosen.

a. _____

b. _____

c. _____

Step 2 Discuss the topics one at a time. During the discussions, try to get the members of the group to get off the topic by digressing. Be sure to use expressions to introduce your digressions.

Step 3 If you are successful and get the group to listen to your digression, you can also practice using appropriate expressions to return to the main point.

SKILL B

Asking for Information, Seeking Confirmation, and Challenging with Tag Questions

Tag questions are questions added or "tagged on" at the end of a statement. They are very short, usually consisting of only a subject and an auxiliary verb.

Affirmative and Negative Tag Questions

1. If the statement is negative, the tag question is always affirmative.

                                  negative   affirmative

example: He's not coming to soccer practice today, is he?

2. If the statement is affirmative, generally the tag question is negative.

                                 affirmative   negative

example: He's coming to soccer practice today, isn't he?

3. But sometimes an affirmative statement is followed by an affirmative tag question.

                                 affirmative   affirmative

example: He's coming to soccer practice today, is he?

Intonation plays a big part in conveying the intention of a tag question. The first two examples of tag questions above might be genuine questions with rising intonation. These same tag questions could easily be changed to rhetorical questions by using falling intonation. Try it.

The third example is a challenging question (an affirmative statement with an affirmative tag question) with a sudden rising intonation.

Tag questions are used for three purposes.

Purposes of Tag Questions

1. *As genuine questions*
Here the speaker sincerely wants to know the answers. The genuine tag question has rising intonation.

example: You're coming to soccer practice today, aren't you?

2. *As rhetorical questions*
Here the speaker knows the answer already and just wants confirmation or agreement from the listener. The rhetorical question has falling intonation.

example: You're not wearing your new shoes, are you?

3. *As challenging questions*
The speaker uses an affirmative statement followed by an affirmative tag to signal a challenge meaning: "You're (he's, she's, they're) not going to get away with that." The challenging tag question has rising intonation, but it rises more suddenly than the genuine question.

example: So they think they're going to win the match, do they?

Conversations

Listen to the following conversations that include tag questions.

conversation 1 Steven is telling Tom about the first soccer practice of the season, which is only two days away. Listen to the speakers and answer the question.

What intonation pattern does Steven use—genuine question, rhetorical question, or challenging question?

_____

conversation 2 Steven and Tom have been looking forward to playing soccer on Saturday all week. Steven is telling a third friend, George, about the practice. Listen to the speakers and answer the question.

What intonation pattern does Steven use this time—genuine question, rhetorical question, or challenging question?

_____

conversation 3 Soccer practice has been arranged for 6:30 A.M. because another team has reserved the field for 8:30. Tom and Steven are talking about Karl, who told Tom that he wouldn't be coming until eight. Listen to the speakers and answer the question.

What intonation pattern does Steven use here—genuine question, rhetorical question, or challenging question?

_____

conversation 4 Charlie's boss expects a report on Friday but realizes that it would be useful at a meeting on Wednesday. Listen to the speakers and answer the question.

What intonation pattern does the boss use—genuine question, rhetorical question, or challenging question?

_____

conversation 5 Josie comes home and sees Peter, one of her housemates, sitting in the living room with his feet up. Since it's already six o'clock, she concludes that it's not his turn to cook. Listen to the speakers and answer the question.

What single-word tag questions are used in this conversation?

_____

Listen In

Step 1 Listen to the lecture again. This time, notice the tag questions. As you listen, fill in the following chart. The first one is done as an example.

Step 2 When you are finished, compare your chart with those of your classmates. If there are differences, listen to the lecture again and see if you can agree this time.

The lecturer claims that even ants are more productive in the presence of their peers

	genuine	**rhetorical**	**challenging**
Affirmative	_____	_____	_____
	_____	_____	_____
	_____	_____	_____
Negative	*don't you*	_____	_____
	_____	_____	_____
	_____	_____	_____
	_____	_____	_____
	_____	_____	_____
Other	_____	_____	_____
	_____	_____	_____
	_____	_____	_____

Speak Out

Native English speakers tend to use tag questions much more than nonnative English speakers. Do the following activities to practice getting confirmation using tag questions.

activity 1

In groups of five to ten, get confirmation from one person at a time about his or her leisure activities. For practice, use only statements followed by tag questions to do this. If you are unsure or if you really have no idea what this person does during his or her leisure time, make an educated guess followed by a genuine tag question (with rising intonation). If you definitely know one of this person's leisure-time activities, you may make a statement followed by a rhetorical tag question.

When this person has answered all the tag questions on this topic the group can think of, it's time to get confirmation from another member of the group, and so on. Here are a few examples:

- You like to play handball, don't you?

    or

    You don't like to play handball, do you?

- You're a terrific dancer, aren't you?

    or

    You don't like to dance, do you?

- Your collection of jazz records is the largest in your city, isn't it?

    or

    You don't collect jazz records, do you?

activity 2

Step 1 In groups of two to four, role play the following scenarios or devise some scenarios of your own. Use as many tag questions—and types of tag questions—as you can during your role plays. Then present your role plays to the class.

Step 2 Keep score of the number of genuine, rhetorical, and challenging tag questions each group uses. You might give bonus points for using challenging tags in the role plays because these can be quite tricky to use appropriately.

group no.	genuine	rhetorical	challenging
___ ___	___ ___	___ ___	___ ___
___ ___	___ ___	___ ___	___ ___
___ ___	___ ___	___ ___	___ ___

Step 3 Total up the scores for each group. Which group used the most tag questions?

_____

Which group used the most types of tag questions? _____

Which group used the most "challenging" tag questions? _____

SCENARIOS

1. During intermission at a concert with friends, half the group thinks the concert is awful and wants to leave; the other half thinks it's wonderful and wants to stay.

2. A teenager who was supposed to be home by midnight arrives home at 3:00 A.M. The teenager doesn't want to be grounded (a punishment in which the young person can't leave the house except to go to school), so he or she tries to tiptoe quietly into the house. One of the parents, however, has come downstairs for a snack, and the teenager and the parent bump right into each other.

3. At a restaurant, some friends are deciding whether to split the bill equally, have each person pay exactly her or his share, or let one person have a turn paying the whole thing.

4. On your vacation you take an airplane to _____ . You try to start a conversation with the attractive person next to you, but a naughty child is making a lot of noise and keeps interrupting you. The parent doesn't seem to be anywhere around.

5. You and some friends are on a mountain camping trip. Although you had planned to stay for five days, it's starting to snow on the second day.

6. At the office, the boss has suggested a ten-hour day, with a four-day work week. The employees may make the final decision, but some of them like to have long weekends, and others prefer to spread out their leisure time over the entire week.

7. At home, you've just received a phone call saying that you've won an all-expenses-paid vacation to Hawaii. You may bring one friend. Your two best friends were sitting with you when you received the call.

You will hear two conversations. After each conversation, you will hear a question. To answer the question, read the four possible answers and decide which one is the best answer. Circle the letter of the best answer.

CONVERSATION 1

A. On a tennis court.
B. On a racquetball court.
C. In a sporting goods store.
D. On a golf course.

CONVERSATION 2

A. Tom doesn't have many people on his side.
B. Tom can't possibly win the election.
C. Tom will win if the special interest groups vote for him.
D. Tom is certain to win the election.

CHAPTER ten

Crime and Punishment

in this chapter

You will hear a lecture titled "Choice: The Uniquely Human Problem." It discusses what it means to have freedom of choice and how this applies to the topic of crime and punishment.

Skill A—Learning Strategy: Paraphrasing

Skill B—Language Function: Expressing Wishes, Hopes, and Desires

- On December 1, 1955, Rosa Parks, a 42-year-old seamstress, chose to break the law in Montgomery, Alabama. She was ordered by a city bus driver to give up her seat to a white man, as was then required by the city's racial segregation laws. She refused and was arrested. Four days later, the black community, led by Dr. Martin Luther King, Jr., began a boycott of the city bus company that lasted 382 days. Then the U.S. Supreme Court ruled that segregation on city buses was unconstitutional. For her role in sparking the successful boycott, Rosa Parks became known as the "mother of the civil rights movement."

- The longest known prison sentence ever given out by a judge was 141,078 years. A Thai woman and seven associates each received this sentence in Bangkok Criminal Court in 1989. Their crime: swindling the public through a fake deposit-taking business.

- Recent studies of the death penalty in the United States show that, contrary to expectations, states which use the death penalty as capital punishment for the crime of murder have higher murder rates than states which do not use it.

Getting Started

Sharing Your Experience

Get in groups of three to complete the following activities. Since some of your responses might reflect cultural differences, try to form groups with people from several different cultural backgrounds.

**activity 1**

Do you know people who have considered doing something they knew was wrong in order to get something they wanted? (They might have thought about pretending to be sick in order to get a day off or taking something from a store without paying for it.) What did they consider doing? Did they actually follow through with their idea? Was any punishment eventually involved? Share one or two stories with the whole class.

activity 2

In the first column below, list several things that are against the law. Next to each illegal act, list the punishment that is usually given for breaking this law. Then talk about these crimes and punishments. Which ones do you think are fair? Which ones are not? Why not? Share the key points of your small-group discussions with the whole class.

THE CRIME	THE PUNISHMENT
_____	_____
_____	_____
_____	_____
_____	_____
_____	_____
_____	_____

activity 3

Now think about some everyday social actions that are not against the laws of the country but are against some people's personal codes of conduct. (For example, someone may not approve of another person's smoking, or they may feel that students shouldn't help each other with homework.) List some of these "crimes" below along with the usual "punishments." Which ones do you think are fair? Which ones are not? Why not? Share the key points of your small-group discussions with the whole class.

THE "CRIME"	THE "PUNISHMENT"
_____	_____
_____	_____
_____	_____
_____	_____
_____	_____
_____	_____

Vocabulary

To introduce you to some of the concepts used in the lecture, rewrite the following sentences in your own words. Do not use your dictionary. Try to get the meaning from the sentence and make an educated guess. Then compare answers with your classmates. You may want to check in a dictionary if there are important differences among the answers.

example: "The unexamined life is not worth living."
—*Socrates*

If you don't look closely at your own behavior, your life will be meaningless.

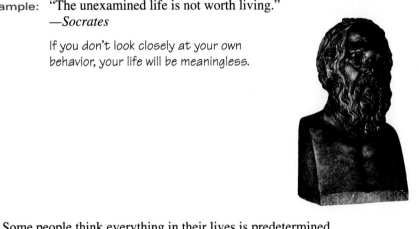

1. Some people think everything in their lives is predetermined.

   _____

   _____

2. Our genetic makeup programs us to do the things we do.

   _____

   _____

3. He has a pessimistic view of the future of the world.

   _____

   _____

4. She has an optimistic attitude toward life.

   _____

   _____

5. The practical implications of choice intensify when life or death decisions have to be made.

   _____

   _____

6. He was found not guilty "by reason of insanity."

_____

_____

7. We only punish people who choose consciously and willfully to commit crimes.

_____

_____

Match each of the following vocabulary words with the best definition. Then look up each word in the dictionary to see if you guessed right.

1. _____ remorse

2. _____ condemnation

3. _____ criteria

4. _____ mundane

5. _____ violation

a. ordinary
b. disapproval or criticism
c. regret for doing something wrong
d. standards for judgment
e. infraction, illegality

SKILL **A**
Paraphrasing

In the first vocabulary exercise in this chapter you were asked to rewrite sentences in your own words. We call this rewriting *paraphrasing,* and it can be a useful study skill. In almost every class you are certain to be asked to restate in your own words something the instructor said or that you read in your textbook. Paraphrasing is similar to summarizing, but a paraphrase is about the same length as the original material; a summary is much shorter than the original material.

Listen In

Listen to the lecture once all the way through for the main ideas.

exercise 2 Listen to the lecture again and paraphrase the following sections. Your teacher will stop the tape after each section, but you still may want to jot down a few notes while you listen to help you remember the ideas presented.

1. Listen closely to the section about Hindu and Buddhist beliefs in karma and reincarnation. Both these views are said to have important effects on our lives. Now paraphrase this section.

On the Buddhist Wheel of Life are the snake (anger), the pig (greed), and the rooster (ignorance), representing the causes of our poor choices.

_____

_____

_____

_____

_____

_____

2. Listen carefully to the views presented about decisions involving criminal offenses. The example given is of a judge sentencing a person to prison for violation of certain rules in a community. Now paraphrase this section.

_____

_____

_____

_____

_____

3. Listen carefully to the views presented on criminals who escape punishment for their actions. Now paraphrase this section.

_____

_____

_____

_____

4. Listen carefully to the list of everyday choices we all have to make (near the end of the lecture), followed by the professor's final comments. Now paraphrase this section.

_____

_____

_____

_____

 exercise 3 Listen to the whole lecture once again to check your work. Then share your work with your classmates by reading it aloud. How did your paraphrasing differ from your classmates'?

Speak Out

You may have heard this quotation: "You can never say 'yes' to something without saying 'no' to something else." Real-life situations often force us to make unpleasant choices and to give up things we want.

 **activity**

Step 1 Work in groups of three or four. Only one person in the group looks at the textbook. This person reads one of the following problem situations silently and then paraphrases it for the group. (Do not mention the possible solutions given in the book at this time.)

Step 2 All group members then clarify what the problem is and discuss what they would do about it. They can also talk about why they would choose a certain solution.

Step 3 The first person then reads aloud the possible solutions given in the book. Then the group discusses the pros and cons of any of these solutions that group members did not mention earlier.

Step 4 Another person takes the textbook, chooses another problem from the list, and repeats steps 1 through 3 with the group.

PROBLEM SITUATIONS

1. You're having dinner with an American family. Everything goes well until they bring in the main course: pork chops with apples. You don't eat pork.

    Would you:
    a. tell them you're not hungry
    b. explain why you don't eat pork
    c. eat the meal
    d. tell them why they should not eat pork
    e. leave
    f. other

2. You are standing in the checkout line in a drugstore when you notice a person in the line next to you taking two small bottles of perfume out of the shopping basket and placing them into a coat pocket.

    Would you:
    a. tell the person to pay for them
    b. tell the checkout clerk what just happened
    c. clear your throat and stare at the person
    d. ignore the situation
    e. other

3. The subject matter for a course you are taking is extremely difficult. Your friend, who took the same course last semester, says that the final is absolutely impossible but that you might pass it with a little "help"—that is, if you are told what will be on the test.

Would you:
a. let your friend give you the answers to the test
b. let your friend give you some hints but not tell you all the answers
c. not accept any help from your friend
d. other

4. You work in a large computer corporation and are in charge of hiring new employees. You must choose a new office manager from two candidates. One is a long-time friend who is new to the company; the other is a first-rate worker who has been with the company for eight years.

Would you:
a. offer your friend the position
b. offer the proven employee the job
c. other

5. The speed limit on the highway is posted at 55 mph. All the other cars around you are going at least 65 or 70 mph, so you decide to move along with the rest of the traffic at about 68 mph. All of a sudden you hear a siren and see the swirling blue lights of a highway patrol car behind you. You pull over to the side of the road, with the highway patrol car right behind you. The patrol officer asks you why you were going so fast. What will you say?

a. I thought it was OK because everyone else was doing it.
b. Why did you stop me? That guy in the Corvette was going even faster.
c. I'm sorry. I'm a foreigner and I don't understand the laws here.
d. other

SKILL **B**

Expressing Wishes, Hopes, and Desires

The lecturer in this chapter wants his students to seriously consider both the choices they make and the underlying reasons for these choices. He uses certain expressions to indicate wishes, hopes, and desires during the lecture.

Some Ways to Express Wishes, Hopes, and Desires	
I wish . . .	I want . . .
If only . . .	I could use . . .
I hope . . .	I need . . .

Conversations

Listen to the following conversation, which includes expressions of wishes, hopes, and desires. Write down all the expressions you hear. Compare notes with your classmates.

_____

_____

_____

_____

_____

_____

Listen In

Read items 1 to 6 here and on page 126 before you listen to the lecture once more. Then listen for the expressions in the lecture and complete the sentences, using your own words to paraphrase the lecturer. Stop the tape to write if necessary.

1. The lecturer *hopes* the students remember _____

_____

2. He *wants* to present a few more ideas on _____

_____

3. The lecturer asks the students how many of them have looked at their past actions and said, "*I wish* _____."

   Or "*If only* _____."

4. The lecturer does not want to focus on the light sentence aspect of the Hinckley case; he *wants* _____

   _____

5. In summary, he *hopes* the lecture _____

   _____

6. All of us *could use* _____

   _____

Speak Out

activity **1**

Think about how you would complete the following sentences. Then share your answers with a partner or in small groups.

1. I wish I were . . .
2. All I really need is . . .
3. If only I had . . .
4. I want to make better choices in my life. I hope to do this by . . .

activity **2**

Situations often come up in which you must express your hopes and desires or ask for what you want. This sometimes requires care on your part so that you do not appear impolite. Role play the following three scenarios with a partner. Use a variety of expressions to politely explain your wishes. Pick one scenario to present to the whole class.

1. You have signed up for a course that you've been hoping to take for a long time, but you just haven't had the time or the money to do it until now. The instructor begins the first day by asking you to tell her or him what you hope to get from the course.

2. Lucky you! You have been selected for a job interview for a position as a translator at the United Nations (or a job of your choice). The interviewer asks what you hope to gain from your experience as a translator and you answer. Then ask the interviewer what qualities she or he hopes to find in an employee.

3. Your friend is twenty-three years old today, and you are planning a surprise birthday party. Your guests will arrive at 6:00 P.M. It's 5:30 P.M., and you realize that you have no ice. You run to your nearby supermarket to get the ice. Unfortunately, there are ten people in line ahead of you. It looks like you're going to be late for your own party. What might your hopes and wishes be in this situation? Turn and express your thoughts to the person in line next to you.

activity 3

In a small groups, role play the following scenario, with each person taking a different role and expressing the wishes and hopes of the various people involved. You can use phrases like these:

I wish . . .	He needs . . .
I hope . . .	If only he . . .
If only he had/hadn't . . .	He could use . . .

Charles Burke is on trial for murder. He was a wonderful child and did well in school. At nineteen he was drafted into the army and was sent to fight in Vietnam. Two years later he returned home and tried to pick up where he'd left off, but things were never quite the same again for Charles.

He was thrown out of school for fighting with a professor. He was fired from several jobs. He wanted to meet a nice girl and get married, but he couldn't seem to get close to anyone. Finally, one day Charles shot someone for "no reason."

Charles's lawyer hopes that Charles will not be held responsible for his crime. He hopes that the judge and jury will understand that Charles was "temporarily insane" and did not consciously choose to commit murder.

The following characters are being interviewed by CNN:

- Charles Burke
- Charles's lawyer
- the prosecuting attorney
- Charles mother (or father)
- the wife of the murdered man

- Charles's best friend from school
- Charles's kindly grade school teacher
- the judge
- a dismissed jury member

focus on testing

You will hear two conversations. After each conversation, you will hear a question. To answer the question, read the four possible answers and decide which one is the best answer. Circle the letter of the best answer.

CONVERSATION 1

A. If you want to commit a crime, don't tell me about it.
B. If you want to steal a car, don't go to jail.
C. If you aren't ready to take the consequences, don't do it.
D. If you commit a crime, you can't get caught.

CONVERSATION 2

A. You should believe what older people tell you.
B. There might be a bad side to getting what you wish for.
C. You will probably become famous someday.
D. You will be very disappointed if you don't get what you wish for.

The Physical World

You will hear a lecture called "Penguins at the Pole." In the lecture you will learn some fascinating and surprising facts about the habits of these unusual birds.

Skill A—Learning Strategy: Outlining

Skill B—Language Function: Stating Reasons

DID YOU KNOW?

- **The first people to reach the South Pole were five Norwegian men led by Captain Amundsen on December 4, 1911. They traveled fifty-five days by dog sled to get there.**

- **The first people to reach the North Pole were three Russian explorers who arrived and departed by air on April 23, 1968.**

- **The North and South Polar Regions balance the flow of air and water for the entire planet. Without this balance, we could face catastrophic floods and droughts that would change the face of the earth. Substantial melting of ice at the poles would turn Nevada deserts into oceanfront property.**

Getting Started
Sharing Your Experience

Get into groups of three to do the following discussion activity.

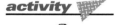

Imagine that you are a zoologist about to begin a study of penguins with two other scientists. To prepare for your field study, which will include trips to the polar regions, discuss the following questions with your colleagues. Write your answers in the following chart.

questions	answers
1. What facts about penguins would you want to learn to prepare for the trip?	
2. Who would you take with you and why?	
3. What supplies would you need?	
4. Where would you go first? Why?	
5. How would you get to your destination?	
6. How much time do you think you would need?	
7. What are the dangers you would face?	
8. At what times of day would you make your observations? Why?	

Compare your chart with those of other groups.

Vocabulary

Test your knowledge of the vocabulary words italicized in the following sentences. They will appear in the lecture. If the italicized word is used correctly, mark the sentence C. If it is used incorrectly, mark the sentence I. The first two items are done as examples.

1. _C_ Because I like *desolate* places, I'm thinking of becoming a hermit and moving to an arctic region.

2. _I_ Inland in arctic regions you can find beautiful *beachfront* property.

3. ____ *Catastrophic* floods could change the biological patterns of the world.

4. ____ Most *migratory* birds cannot fly.

5. ____ The term *ecosystem* refers to a network of relationships among organisms that are interdependent.

6. ____ A temperature of 32 degrees *Fahrenheit* is 0 degrees *Celsius*.

7. ____ Birds that *fast* cover a lot of territory in a very short time.

8. ____ Once penguin chicks begin to hatch, the colony begins to *teem* with life.

9. ____ The penguin's *disposition* is black and white.

10. ____ A *ferocious* attack by a sea leopard might kill a penguin.

11. ____ The *brooding* instinct is very strong in penguins.

12. ____ Penguins *engage* in playful activities.

SKILL A

Outlining

Information can be condensed and organized for study by putting it in outline form. Outlining highlights the main ideas and supporting information found in a reading passage or an oral presentation (such as a class lecture). Following is a typical outline format.

I. _____

    A. _____

    B. _____

II. _____

    A. _____

    B. _____

III. _____

    A. _____

        1. _____

        2. _____

    B. _____

This format can vary, depending on how the material is organized. However, the main points are always represented by roman numerals (I, II, etc.), and less important points are represented by capital letters (A, B, etc.). Minor points are represented by arabic numerals (1, 2, etc.).

Listen In

Listen to the lecture on penguins. Pay special attention to the information about mating habits because in Section 2 you will be asked to complete an outline of this section.

Study the partial outline below. Note that the information given in each category starts with a capital letter and has no end punctuation. Then listen to the tape with a partner and fill in the information missing from the outline. Compare your answers with those of your classmates.

I. Mating habits of penguins

    A. Need for order leads penguins to build nests in rows

    B. Order is often interrupted by small "wars" between males

        1. _____

        2. _____

   C. _____

    D. Losers move to edge of nesting ground

exercise **3**   Listen to the lecture again. Pay special attention to the information about brooding. With a partner, complete an outline of that segment of the presentation on the lines below. Be sure to include in your outline (1) the reasons for the high casualty rate of eggs, (2) what happens when chicks hatch, and (3) cooperative parenting activities. Compare your outlines with those of your classmates.

  II. Penguin brooding

_____

_____

_____

_____

_____

_____

_____

_____

_____

_____

_____

_____

_____

_____

Speak Out

In the ecosystem discussed in the lecture, penguins are lucky in one way: Their major enemy, the sea leopard, does not use high technology to hunt them. This is not true for some of the creatures that people hunt. For example, the use of high technology to kill whales has caused worldwide controversy. Discuss the following questions:

1. Why are whales hunted? What parts of the whale are used?
2. What methods are used to hunt whales?
3. What is Greenpeace? What does it do?

Now decide what *your* position is on the following issues.

The Greenpeace boat *Zodiac* approaches a Soviet whaler in an effort to stop the killing of sperm whales

1. Are the methods used to hunt whales acceptable or not?
2. Should governments control the way in which whales are hunted? The way in which all creatures are hunted?
3. Should whales and other endangered species be protected?
4. Do you support the philosophy of Greenpeace? Its methods?

Present your views to your classmates and explain why you feel this way. A brief outline will help you organize your thoughts. Your position on each issue is a main idea and should be listed after a roman numeral. Under the roman numeral, other less important information that supports each main idea can be listed after capital letters and arabic numerals.

SKILL B

Stating Reasons

The lecture in this chapter contains words used to emphasize the reasons why penguins exhibit certain behaviors—why they do what they do. These words are also commonly used in everyday conversations to emphasize the reasons for things.

Words Used to State Reasons		
because (of)	on account of this	since
for this reason	in view of that fact	seeing as how
the reason is (that)	owing to	(very informal)

Conversations

Listen to the following conversation, which contains several different ways of stating reasons. List all the expressions used to state reasons on the following lines. Compare your list with your classmates' lists.

_____

_____

_____

Listen In

Listen to the lecture again. Notice how certain words make it easy for you to pick out the reasons being given. Then use one of the expressions below to complete each of the following sentences. When you are finished, compare answers with those of your classmates.

because	owing to
because of	in view of that fact
since	for this reason
on account of	

1. The polar regions are unique among the regions of the earth _____ even though they are cold and desolate, they influence the world's climates enormously.

2. _____ the polar regions are icy deserts, only hardy forms of life can survive there.

3. _____ it is quite odd that the penguin chose this land as home.

4. The penguins can fast for some time _____ they have fed constantly up to that point.

5. They have the energy to swim the hundreds of miles they must travel _____ their previous feeding.

6. _____ many birds converge at the same time, order and tidiness are needed.

7. Mates treat each other graciously, perhaps _____ all the struggles they have endured before mating.

8. _____ these struggles, some penguins are injured.

9. _____ the penguin's good nature, they often share childcare.

10. The sea leopard successfully attacks penguins. _____ the group is smaller when it returns to the mating ground.

Speak Out

activity

Zoos and wild animal parks provide people in urban areas with the opportunity to observe remote ecosystems. To practice the words you studied in the previous exercises, do one of the following activities in small groups.

1. If you have been to a zoo or wild animal park, describe it to your classmates. Use the words for stating reasons on page 134 and answer these questions:
   a. Why do you think the zoo or park was built?
   b. Why did you go there?
   c. Why do most people go there?
   d. Are the animals well cared for?
   e. Do you think the animals are content, or do you think they suffer because they are not in the wild? Why?

Hosts and guests at a wild animal park in Texas

2. If you have not been to a zoo or animal park, are you in favor of or against zoos or wild animal parks? Tell why, using at least three of the expressions for stating reasons from Skill B.

activity

Now that you've heard the presentation on penguins, consider again your imaginary field study of penguins. Discuss why you would or would not like to take such a trip, using the expressions suggested in Skill B. What facts about penguins would you want to learn before the trip? What specific behaviors would you want to watch for and why?

focus on testing

You will hear two conversations. After each conversation, you will hear a question. To answer the question, read the four possible answers and decide which one is the best answer. Circle the letter of the best answer.

CONVERSATION 1

A. A teaching job at Elmhurst College.
B. A chance to join the Antarctica expedition.
C. A chance to join another expedition.
D. To be cut from the teaching staff at the college.

CONVERSATION 2

A. People in the polar regions are in danger.
B. People should pay more attention to polar bears.
C. The ecology of the polar regions is important to everyone.
D. People who live near the polar regions are not ecologists.

CHAPTER twelve

Together on a Small Planet

You will listen to a lecture in a course in popular culture called "Folk Wisdom." The lecture shows how several famous Americans used humorous stories to help people live better lives and get along better with each other.

Skill A—Learning Strategy: Summarizing

Skill B—Language Function: Telling a Joke

137

DID YOU KNOW?

- Someone surveyed Americans and found that 85% of them thought they had a "good sense of humor."

- North Americans almost always give a brief apology or introduction before telling a joke. These apologies are called "disclaimers." The average number of disclaimers made before telling a joke is 1.9 for men and 3.4 for women.

- When the comedian Henny Youngman stands up and tells jokes for 40 minutes, he averages 245 jokes. That's about 6 jokes a minute.

Getting Started

Sharing Your Experience

activity

Get into small groups for short discussions. Each group should choose a secretary to take notes and give a short report to the class when the discussions are through.

1. Most cultures pass on their folk wisdom through humorous sayings that children learn as they grow up. "Don't bite the hand that feeds you" and "Look before you leap" are two common English proverbs. Think of similar sayings in your own native language. Translate them into English and share them with your group. Do other people in your group find these saying humorous?

2. Think of advice that your mother, father, grandparents, or perhaps a wise uncle or aunt has given to you. Share this advice with your group. Is any of this advice humorous? If so, why do you think so? Can you explain what makes it funny?

3. Describe your impressions of humor from other cultures. What makes people in other cultures laugh? Do people laugh mostly at real events or at made-up jokes? What subjects make people laugh? Is the humor mainly verbal, or is a lot of it visual?

4. Are teachers who get students to laugh more effective in helping students learn? Why or why not?

Never put off until tomorrow what you can do the day after tomorrow. MARK TWAIN

Vocabulary

By now you know that English words may have multiple meanings. Look over the following list of words to see how they will be used in the lecture in this chapter.

ain't	*nonstandard English contraction of* am not, is not, *or* are not
chastity	*restraint, modesty, and purity*
colloquial	*characteristic of informal rather than formal English*
conscience	*feeling of moral responsibility*
folly	*foolishness*
hain't	*nonstandard English contraction of* has *or* have not
impromptu	*made or done without planning, spontaneous*
moralist	*a person who comments on what is right and wrong*
pretension	*an air of inviting admiration or an act intended to make one seem better than one really is (in terms of class or morals)*
vanity	*excessive pride, egotism*

 Now apply these definitions by choosing the sentence in which the italicized word is used correctly. The first one is done as an example.

1. folly
   a. _____ A student's *folly* will probably help the student make friends.
   b. _____ Generally, people see the *folly* right after summer when the leaves turn red and gold.
   c. __X__ A friend may sometimes help us see the *folly* of our ways.

2. chastity
   a. _____ The little girl in the white dress, ribbons in her hair, her hands folded in her lap, and her eyes cast down, is the perfect picture of *chastity.*
   b. _____ He left his *chastity* on the counter at the bank.
   c. _____ Many people donate money to a favorite *chastity* at Christmas time.

3. moralist
   a. _____ The advice of a *moralist* can be helpful and at the same time quite annoying.
   b. _____ A *moralist* is someone who always takes a second serving of food at dinner.
   c. _____ The ecological study of the moors in England was done by a qualified *moralist.*

4. colloquial
   a. _____ His *colloquial* dress made him stand out from the rest of the group.
   b. _____ His manner of speaking was very *colloquial,* but since this was a very informal situation it was quite all right.
   c. _____ He was known to everyone in town as a *colloquial* character.

5. pretension

    a. _____ He went from city to city searching for the best *pretension*.

    b. _____ She made elaborate *pretensions* to being generous, but when her friends or relatives asked her for money, she always refused.

    c. _____ Your friends will appreciate it if you pay *pretension* when they are speaking to you.

6. conscience

    a. _____ The idea was very *conscience,* not at all abstract.

    b. _____ His *conscience* was aching, so his wife gave him an aspirin.

    c. _____ His *conscience* told him to turn in the $500 he picked up in front of the cafeteria to the lost and found department.

7. vanity

    a. _____ *Vanity* is something parents try to develop in their children.

    b. _____ The *vanity* in his neck stuck out whenever he got angry.

    c. _____ His *vanity* was unbelievable! He looked at himself in every window as he walked down the street.

8. impromptu

    a. _____ He got up early and put on an *impromptu* robe.

    b. _____ Most people believe making an *impromptu* speech is difficult.

    c. _____ He stayed up late at night and got up early every morning, leading an *impromptu* life.

SKILL

Summarizing

Consider these situations:

- You have just read an excellent book and want to tell a friend about it.
- You have seen a thrilling movie and want to persuade your instructor to go see it.
- You have heard a fantastic lecture and want to share your newfound knowledge with a roommate.

How can you best convey this type of information? You could tell everything you remember about the book, movie, or lecture, but you will probably just select the major points or highlights and tell these to your listener. This is called summarizing. Throughout this book you have been developing skills to help you summarize. For example, you have learned to

- listen for the main idea
- listen for key terms
- outline
- paraphrase

To create a good summary—one that is both accurate and concise—you need to follow two steps:

1. Gather information by reading, taking notes, or listening carefully for the main points or highlights.
2. Organize your thoughts carefully so that your summary is as brief as possible but still accurate and complete.

Your audience will help you decide how thorough you need to be. If you are presenting your summary to an instructor, keep in mind any clues your instructor might have given you during the lecture to indicate what he or she considers especially important. If you are summarizing a movie for a friend, you can be less thorough. For example, you might describe one scene in detail and skip several important ones. Or you might choose to not give away the surprise ending.

Terms That Signal a Repetition or Summary of Important Points

in sum

in summary

to sum up

to summarize

Part of the task of summarizing is knowing what to include and what to leave out. For example,

- There is no need to summarize jokes, interruptions, or other digressions in a lecture.
- Generally, you should not try to summarize a short quotation. If the quotation is carefully worded and states a main point, your summary could end up being longer than the original quotation.

Listen In

exercise

Listen to the lecture once to get the main ideas. Then listen again and take notes. After that, write a short summary about the following people, including information about their lifestyles and humorous sayings. Share and discuss your responses with your classmates.

1. Benjamin Franklin

_____

_____

_____

_____

_____

_____

2. Abraham Lincoln

_____

_____

_____

_____

_____

_____

_____

_____

_____

_____

3. Mark Twain

_____

_____

_____

_____

_____

_____

_____

_____

_____

_____

Speak Out

When completed, each of the sayings below should sum up a way of looking at life. In small groups, think of various ways of completing each sentence. When you have finished all nine, choose one or two of the group's favorites to share with the class. The first one is done as an example.

1. Two people can keep a secret if . . .

    example: . . . one lives on a houseboat in Antarctica and the other lives in Siberia, and neither one has a telephone or mail service.

2. People will forgive others anything except . . .

_____

_____

3. If you want something done well . . .

_____

_____

4. There are three kinds of teachers . . .

_____

_____

5. There are only three things necessary to keep your wife happy . . .

_____

_____

6. There are only three things necessary to keep your husband happy . . .

_____

_____

7. When angry, count to four; when very angry . . .

_____

_____

8. Sometimes I feel as out of place as . . .

_____

_____

9. Every person with an idea also has . . .

_____

_____

activity 2

Read the following quotations. In groups of two to four, devise brief miniplays that illustrate the main ideas of the quotations. Don't tell the rest of the class which quotation you are acting out. Allow the class to guess which quotation best summarizes your skit.

1. "Everyone is ignorant—only on different subjects." —*Will Rogers*

2. "Everything is funny as long as it's happening to someone else." —*Will Rogers*

3. "Do not do unto others as you . . . (want them to) do unto you. Their tastes may not be the same" —*G. B. Shaw*

4. "A loving person lives in a loving world. A hostile person lives in a hostile world: Everyone you meet is your mirror." —*Ken Keyes, Jr.*

5. "I believe I found the missing link between animal and civilized man. It is us." —*Konrad Lorenz*

6. "The worst sin towards our fellow creatures is not to hate them, but to be indifferent to them; that's the essence of inhumanity." —*G. B. Shaw*

7. "I've known a lot of troubles in my time—and most of them never happened." —*Mark Twain*

8. "You can look at a cup as being either half empty or half full." —*proverb*

9. "A bore is a man who, when you ask him how he is, tells you." —*Burt Leston Taylor*

10. "Better to be quarreling than lonesome." —*Irish proverb*

SKILL B

Telling a Joke

How to Introduce a Joke

Humor is valued in English-speaking countries, and it is common to hear your doctor, dentist, teacher, friends, or acquaintances tell jokes. Sharing laughter is a good way to put other people at ease and help create harmony on this small planet of ours.

People usually clearly indicate when they are about to tell a joke. Lecturers often do this so that the audience can just relax and listen and not worry about taking notes.

Conversations

You will hear a group of students who are taking a break, sitting in the student union, hanging out, and telling jokes. As you listen, notice how the students introduce the four jokes they tell. Then answer the question.

1. Catherine tells a joke that she heard her teacher tell.

How does Catherine introduce the joke?

_____

2. Jimmy tells a joke about a boy in New York City.

How does Jimmy introduce his joke?

_____

3. Joanna tells a joke about a man in a restaurant.

How does Joanna introduce her joke?

_____

4. Frank tells a joke about a little girl.

How does Frank introduce the joke?

_____

Listen In

Listen to the lecturer again. Because the lecturer uses quotations from famous people and not jokes, he does not indicate when the humor is coming with comments such as "Let me tell you the one about." However, he does pause and change the rhythm or pace of his speaking.

When you listen to the lecture, try to be aware of pauses and changes in rhythm and pace. Use these cues to help you pay close attention to the humor and the quotations. Write down key words in the quotations so that you can repeat them and possibly use them in your conversations later. To help you, the first five words are given. Use short forms and abbreviations where possible. The first one is done as an example.

Quotations

FRANKLIN

1. *"Early to bed and early to . . ."*

   <u>rise makes a man healthy, wealthy, and wise.</u>

   _____

2. *"Keep your eyes wide open . . ."*

   _____

   _____

3. *"Three may keep a secret . . ."*

   _____

   _____

4. *"If you want a thing . . ."*

   _____

   _____

5. *"There never was a good . . ."*

   _____

   _____

CROCKETT

6. *"Make sure you're right, then . . ."*

   _____

   _____

LINCOLN

7. *"You can fool all of . . ."*

_____

_____

8. *"The Lord prefers common-looking people . . ."*

_____

_____

TWAIN

9. *"Hain't we got all the . . ."*

_____

_____

10. *"There are three kinds of . . ."*

_____

_____

11. *"The reports of my death . . ."*

_____

_____

Speak Out

activity 1

Do you know someone who is almost always funny? Most of us do. And most of us enjoy being around people like this because they encourage us to laugh at the world and at ourselves. In groups, answer the following questions.

1. Who is your favorite comedian?
2. What is so funny about this person?
3. How can a joke be delivered effectively? Ineffectively?

activity 2

Come to class prepared to tell two jokes that you think are very funny. You might want to try them out on some of your friends before telling them in class.

Charlie Chaplin, a comic actor with universal appeal

**activity**

Divide into groups of four or five. Your teacher will assign a topic and ask you to talk together for ten minutes. Possible topics include work, school, sports, dating, marriage, children, politics, or television. As often as possible, include a joke or folk saying in your conversation. When the time is up, share your group's best jokes and sayings with the rest of the class.

focus on testing

You will hear two conversations. After each conversation, you will hear a question. To answer the question, read the four possible answers and decide which one is the best answer. Circle the letter of the best answer.

CONVERSATION 1

A. Because she doesn't like animals.
B. Because his jokes are old and silly.
C. Because she doesn't like Norman.
D. Because she wants to take a coffee break.

CONVERSATION 2

A. If you're not sure about saying something, don't say it.
B. Mr. Leonard might not like the story.
C. Harold doesn't know how to tell a funny story.
D. Don't doubt yourself.

1. Zero, because 0 times *anything* is 0.
2. The answer will be 111,111,111 no matter which digit is used.
3. Mary is only 5 years old and cannot reach the button for the twelfth floor.
4. None. Pigs can't talk.
5. The letter *m*.
6. Just divide the answer by 4 and you will have the number your partner started with.
7. a. The farmer first takes the sheep across the river and leaves it there.
   b. He then returns and takes the lion across the river.
   c. He leaves the lion on the other side and takes the sheep back to the first side.
   d. Then he takes the hay over to the other side and leaves the hay there with the lion.
   e. Finally, he returns for the sheep and the job is done.
8. One. To get the answer, you must draw a family tree. In the tree shown here, the governor is A, his wife is a, and his guest is D.

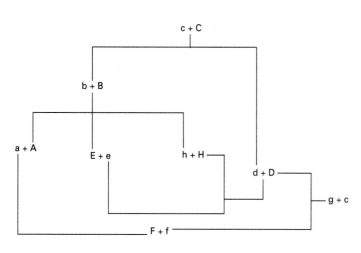

KEY

A = governor of Goleta
a = governor's wife
B = governor's father
b = governor's mother
C = governor's grandfather
c = governor's grandmother
D = governor's father's brother-in-law
d = governor's father's sister
E = governor's brother
e = governor's sister-in-law
F = governor's father-in-law
f = governor's mother-in-law
G = governor's father-in-law's father
g = governor's father-in-law's mother

Tapescript

CHAPTER one

New Challenges

Learning to Speak Someone Else's Language

PROFESSOR: Good morning! I am James Munro, and this is Linguistics 101. Okay, good! It looks like we don't have any lost lambs from the Psych 101 class that's taking place across the hall. Well, now let's get started. Our topic today is "Learning to Speak Someone Else's Language." Before I begin, I'd like to hear some of the questions you may have on this topic. Well, what does this title "Learning to Speak Someone Else's Language" bring to mind? What does it cause you to wonder about? Just call out your questions, and I'll write them down on the overhead.

STUDENT 1: What is language? I mean, where does it come from?

PROFESSOR: Yes, good question. Any others?

STUDENT 2: Who uses language? Is it only humans?

PROFESSOR: Interesting. Next.

STUDENT 3: When does language develop? At what age?

PROFESSOR: Okay, got that. Yes, go ahead.

STUDENT 4: How many languages are there in the world? And can we ever really learn to speak someone else's language?

PROFESSOR: Hmmm. Well, any more? No? Then let's begin with that last question. Can we ever really learn to speak another person's language? I would answer that we must at least try. You see, language is the only window we have for seeing into someone else's mind. But this presents us with a paradox. On the one hand, language can give us an efficient means of communicating with each other and allow us to understand one another and become close. On the other hand, we all know that communication can break down when we don't understand the language, the words, the symbols that someone is using. Okay, so far? And sadly, when communication breaks down, we realize how distant we can be from one another.

Communication can fail even when two people have the same native language. You see, the words and concepts in each person's mind have, in addition to their agreed-upon meanings, very private, personal meanings attached to specific memories and experiences. And perhaps no one else has shared these experiences. Does that make sense to you?

STUDENT 2: I think so. Is it like when I hear the word "dog," I might think of this great little beagle named Sargeant that I had when I was a kid, but my friend, who is afraid of dogs, might think of Cujo? You know, that huge dog that attacked those kids in that old Steven King movie?

PROFESSOR: That's right! Exactly! Here's another example: A rose may be just a beautiful object to me, but to you it may suggest a lovely summer in England, a romantic birthday present, or perhaps an aching back from working in your garden. So you can see the problem, right?

STUDENTS: Sure. Right. Uh-huh.

PROFESSOR: Also, there are between 3,000 and 6,000 public languages in the world—depending on who's counting—and we must add approximately 4 billion private languages since each one of us necessarily has one. Did you get that? Considering these facts, the possibilities for breakdowns in communication seem infinite in number, don't they?

However, we do, in fact, communicate successfully from time to time. And we do learn to speak languages. But learning to speak languages seems to be a very mysterious process. Which brings us back to the first question on our list: Where does language come from? How does it develop?

For a long time, people thought that we learned language only by imitation and association. For example, a baby touches a hot pot and starts to cry. The mother says, "Hot, hot!" and the baby—when it stops crying—imitates the mother and says, "Hot, hot." However, Noam Chomsky, a famous linguist, pointed out that although children do learn some words by imitation and association, they also combine words to make meaningful sentences in ways that are unique, unlearned, and creative. Because young children can make sentences they have never heard before, Chomsky suggested that the ability to learn language is innate—sort of preprogrammed—in human infants. Chomsky meant that underneath all the differences between public and private languages, there is a universal language mechanism that makes it possible for us as infants to learn any language in the world. Are you following me? This theory explains the potential that human infants have for learning language, but it does not really explain how children come to use language in particular ways.

STUDENT 5: Excuse me, Professor. Why do you say that?

PROFESSOR: Chomsky's theories suggest something about the structure, or grammar, of language, but not very much about how language is used. As children develop their language skills, they quickly learn that language is used for more than stating facts such as "The girl is tall." They learn to make requests, to give commands, to agree, to disagree, to explain, to excuse, and even to lie. The uses of language seem endless. As I said earlier, this is the positive side of the paradox. Did you get that?

STUDENTS: Maybe. Not exactly. I'm not sure.

PROFESSOR: In other words, language is a rich means for communicating our intentions to other people who share our native language. And the negative side of the paradox is that not all people speak the same language, and that people who speak other languages seem distant or foreign.

So we're back to where we started. Can we ever really learn to speak someone else's language?

For now, let's assume that we can learn to speak someone else's language—not just a few polite phrases, but really learn to speak it fluently. We know that speaking a language fluently will certainly improve our communication with other speakers of that language, but something else happens as well. I think that learning another language can fundamentally change us as individuals—can change our world view and even our personalities. So then, for example, if we speak French fluently, we can form grammatically correct sentences, of course, but we can also begin to see the world in a way that is typically French. That is, we can view the world from another perspective, and this might change our personalities dramatically. Are you following me?

STUDENT 3: Not exactly. Professor Munro, I'm not sure that I buy the idea that I would actually become someone else just because I learned to speak another language.

PROFESSOR: Okay, consider this. A linguist named Benjamin Lee Whorf took the extreme view that our native language shapes all our perceptions of the world. He claimed that the rules of our native language—for both grammar and usage—can actually determine whatever meaning we find in the world. I believe he meant something like this: Imagine a language that has no words for anger, fear, or jealousy. Will we experience these emotions if we are native speakers of that language? Or, imagine a language that has twenty-five words for love in all its subtle variations. Will we be able to love more deeply if we are native speakers of that language?

STUDENT 3: Well, maybe. But I think there's a real problem with this point of view.

PROFESSOR: Okay. What do you think that might be?

STUDENT 3: Well, for one thing, this point of view ignores the fact that languages change and that they borrow words from other languages. English is an excellent example. The English language regularly takes in words from other languages to better express a thought or name a thing.

PROFESSOR: Yes, of course! As I sat at home writing the notes for this lecture, I looked up at the collage on the wall; I paused to sip a cup of cocoa; I took a bite out of my croissant. Later I experienced a moment of déjà vu—and so forth. In a few sentences I have used four words that have been borrowed from other languages—collage, cocoa, croissant, and déjà vu—because they describe certain things and experiences better than any English words.

STUDENT 3: So English is transformed, or really changed, by words from other languages that express things that really cannot be expressed very well in English?

PROFESSOR: Right! In a way, this is what happens to us when we learn to speak someone else's language. We learn, perhaps, to express things that could not be expressed as well—or even at all—in our own languages. We may learn to understand things in ways that we could not understand them before. Does that make sense to you? We can begin to experience—to get a taste of—what it must be like to be a native speaker of that other language—to be born into another culture.

Oh, my. Our time seems to be up. Next time, come prepared to talk about your own personal experiences in learning about another culture as you learned to speak a second language. Also, please read Chapters One and Two in your textbook and think about this question: If we learn one language so easily as children, why is it such a challenge to learn a second language as adults?

SKILL B   *Offering and Requesting Clarification*

Conversations

Listen to the following speakers. Each of them uses the same expression to try to find out whether the listener is following what has been said.

SPEAKER 1

Mrs. Garcia is talking to a group of employees. Listen to the speaker and answer the questions.

MRS. GARCIA: To figure out the daily costs, you'll have to add up all the numbers in column A, divide by 30, and then multiply by the number of days you'll be there. Is that clear?

Question 1: Which of the expressions in the list above does Mrs. Garcia use?
Question 2: What is her intention when she uses this expression?

Mrs. Smith is talking to her son. Listen to the speaker and answer the question.

MRS. SMITH: No, you can't watch TV. First you have to clean up your room, write a thank-you note to your grandmother for your birthday present, put your bicycle away, take your model airplane project off the kitchen table, put your library books in the car so we can return them tomorrow, finish your homework, and take out the garbage. Is that clear?

Question: Mrs. Smith uses the same expression as Mrs. Garcia. What is Mrs. Smith's intention when she uses this expression?

Focus on Testing

Understanding spoken English on standardized listening comprehension tests (such as the TOEFL) is more difficult than in other contexts. For example, during a standardized test you cannot interact with the speaker to get clarification or rewind the tape to listen again. You get only one chance to listen for important information. The Focus on Testing exercises in this book will help you practice this skill.

You will hear two speakers. After each speaker finishes talking, you will hear a question. To answer the question, read the four possible answers and decide which one is the best answer. Circle the letter of the best answer.

SPEAKER 1

MALE COLLEGE STUDENT: Excuse me, Dr. Jackson. I didn't get that last part. Did you just say that a pun was a kind of play on words?

Question: What does the speaker want to know?

SPEAKER 2

FEMALE PROFESSOR: In different parts of the world, some languages are dying out. In these places, children don't learn to speak their parents' native language. So, as the parents die, their language dies too.

Question: What is the speaker's main point?

CHAPTER two

Looking at Learning

<u>LECTURE AND DISCUSSION</u> *Looking at Learning*

LILIA: Hello. Welcome to the first freshman study-skills class meeting of the semester. I'm Lilia Rothman. I'm a senior in the Education Department and I've been assigned as the T.A. for this group. Has everyone found a comfortable place to sit? There's a chair down here, if you need one.

Okay. Let's get started. Did you know that people spend over half their waking time communicating? They are either writing, reading, speaking, or listening. While I'm passing around the registration cards, think about this: Which activity do you think people do most? Which do you think they do least? Does everybody have a card now? Good.

Well, people seem to spend the least amount of time writing and the most time listening. Did you guess that? Both personal and professional communication depends on the ear. Here's an example. A sales manager for the electronics division of Sylvania Electric Products kept a record of his day and found that he spent 70 or 80 percent of his day on the telephone. One-half of that time was spent listening.

Reading and listening are similar because they're the ways we receive messages. Yet reading and listening are very different in three important ways. First of all, we cannot usually relisten to something as easily as we can reread it. Unless we have a tape recorder, we cannot hear the message again. And what we listen to is not usually written down. The second difference has to do with control of the speed of the message. When we read, we read at a speed we can control. When we listen, the rate or speed of the message is established by the speaker. And third, we must understand the meaning of words and ideas immediately when listening to something or someone. You can't use a dictionary very easily while you're listening.

Now, how fast do people speak and how fast do they listen? People speak English at a rate of about 125 words per minute. People can listen much more quickly than this, though. Actually, people can listen at a rate of 300 words per minute and not lose any comprehension. So it's easy to stop listening for a while, think about your lunch, your upcoming basketball game, or your plans with a boyfriend or girlfriend, and then listen again without losing the gist of what is being said.

But good listeners aren't thinking about their lunch, their basketball game, or their boyfriends or girlfriends—unless, of course, they are listening to their boyfriends or girlfriends. Good listeners do three important things to focus their attention while listening and to keep their minds from wandering.

First, good listeners think ahead of the speaker and try to predict, or guess, what will be said. For example, in a basic science course you may know that the lecturer will follow the textbook. So you say to yourself, "Now he's going to talk about Newton's ideas on motion from Chapter 2 because he's already finished talking about Galileo from Chapter 1." Second, good listeners evaluate what the speaker says. They say to themselves, "That doesn't seem logical," "I can think of a counterexample," or "That must be right; I can think of two more examples." Finally, good listeners review in their minds what has been said.

Now, when you're out there in those big lecture classes you can do more than just listen and follow the three guidelines for good listening. You have the advantage that you can take notes. When you are taking notes you're not likely to lose your focus. You are less likely to daydream. If you take notes, it's easier to review the material in the lecture. And later you may find material and ideas in your notes that you have forgotten since the lecture.

Now, there are two techniques to keep in mind to make your notes more valuable. The first technique is to keep your notes clear and brief. Write in short, uncomplicated sentences. For example, if the lecture is on birds and the lecturer says, "The smallest bird alive is that tiny, but beautiful, hummingbird from Cuba called the bee hummingbird, which is about $2^{1}/_{2}$ inches long," then you might write only "Bee hummingbird is $2^{1}/_{2}$ inches." The second technique is to make a schedule for reviewing notes and actually review them on schedule. For example, you may decide to review your notes every night first thing after dinner. Or you may decide to do it the last thing at night before you go to sleep—or the first thing in the morning. But once you decide, you should stay on schedule.

So . . . on to note-taking. There are two basic systems for note-taking: the thesis/conclusion system and the fact/principle system. The thesis/conclusion system works best with well-organized lectures that have an introduction, a body, and a conclusion. The fact/principle system works best with less-organized lectures. With these lectures you can write the facts on one side of the page, draw a line down the middle, and write the principles on the other side of the page. Then, when you review, you can see if the principles tie together into one main concept or thesis.

Okay let's sum up—does anyone remember the three rules for good listening?

KIM: Um, think ahead of the speaker?

LILIA: Yeah, think ahead of the speaker and try to predict what's coming next. That's one. Who's got another one?

KIM: And you should always evaluate what is being said. You know, decide if it makes sense or not.

LILIA: Right. That's two. Who knows the third rule for good listening? Okay, Kim, go for it. Give us the third one, too.

KIM: I think it's that you should always review what has been said. Maybe say it in your own words in your head.

LILIA: Yes, right! And Kim wins the prize for good listening. Now who remembers the two techniques for note-taking that I talked about?

FAHID: Keep your notes short and on the main point.

LILIA: Right, Fahid. Keep notes brief and to the point. And the second technique?

BILL: Always make time to review your notes. You know, make a schedule and stick to it.

LILIA: Great, Bill! Okay, that's two more good listeners. And last but not least, what are the two systems of note-taking that I presented tonight? What? No one took notes on this? Well, get out some paper now and write this down.

The two systems of note taking are:

1. The thesis/conclusion system
2. The fact/principle system

Great! I can see that you're all setting up your notes in just the right way. And, believe me, you'll get plenty of chances to practice this throughout the term.

Well, that's it for tonight. Please don't forget to hand me your registration cards as you leave. They will help me to learn more of your names before the next session.

Conversations

Listen to the following conversations. Expressions to ask for confirmation are used correctly in some conversations and incorrectly in others. Sometimes the intonation makes the difference.

CONVERSATION 1

At the side of the road, a lost driver is asking a police officer for directions. Listen to the speakers and answer the question. Then discuss your answer with your classmates.

DRIVER: Pardon me. How do I get to the Schubert Theater?

POLICE OFFICER: You make a U-turn, go back on Washington until you hit Jefferson, then make a right turn, and it's the second white building on your left.

DRIVER: Could you repeat that, please?

POLICE OFFICER: Sure. You make a U-turn, go back on Washington until you hit Jefferson, about three blocks, then make a right turn, and it's the second white building on your left.

DRIVER: You mean I turn around and stay on Washington until I get to Jefferson and then make a right?

POLICE OFFICER: Yeah, that's right.

DRIVER: And did you say it's a white building on the left?

POLICE OFFICER: Un-huh.

DRIVER: Thanks a lot.

POLICE OFFICER: You're welcome.

Question: Did the lost driver ask for confirmation appropriately?

CONVERSATION 2

Here is a conversation between a professor and a student. Listen to the speakers and answer the question. Discuss your answer with your classmates.

STUDENT: I didn't get the directions on your test. That's why I did badly.

INSTRUCTOR: Well, Tim, the directions say "Answer 1A and then choose and answer 1B or 1C or 1D."

STUDENT: Do you mean to say that we had to do A and B or C or D?

INSTRUCTOR: Yes, you had a choice for the second half of the question.

STUDENT: Oh, okay.

Question: Did the student respond appropriately?

CONVERSATION 3

Here is a similar conversation between the same professor and student. Listen to the speakers and answer the questions.

STUDENT: Professor Thompson, I'm not sure I understand the directions on this test.

INSTRUCTOR: Well, Tim, the directions say "Answer 1A and then choose and answer 1B or 1C or 1D."

STUDENT: You mean that we all do 1A, but then we each could do any one of B, C, or D?

INSTRUCTOR: That's right, Tim.

STUDENT: Oh, now I see. I won't make that mistake again. Thank you.

Question 1: How do you feel about this student's confirmation strategy?
Question 2: Do your classmates feel the same way? Ask them.

CONVERSATION 4

In this conversation, a student is talking to a secretary about the preregistration procedure. Listen to the speakers and answer the questions. Share your answers with your classmates.

STUDENT: What do I do now?

SECRETARY: You take that white sheet and the blue card. You fill out the white sheet with the courses you want. Then you have your advisor sign the white sheet and the blue card, and you turn them in to the first-floor office in Building Four and pay your fees.

STUDENT: You mean I've got to have my advisor sign both the sheet and the card, and then I've got to stand in line again?

Questions: Would you react the same way if you were this secretary? Why or why not?

CONVERSATION 5

Here is another conversation between a secretary and a student. Listen to the speakers and answer the question. Discuss your answer with your classmates.

STUDENT: Excuse me, could you tell me what I must do next to preregister?

SECRETARY: You take that white sheet and the blue card. You fill out the white sheet with the courses you want. Then you have your advisor sign the white sheet and the blue card, and you turn them in to the first-floor office in Building Four and pay your fees.

STUDENT: I'm not sure I understand. Do you mean that the advisor must sign both forms? And that I take the forms to Building Four and pay my fees there?

SECRETARY: Yes, that's right.

STUDENT: Oh, okay. Now I understand. Thank you.

Question: What is the critical element that makes the difference between conversation 4 and conversation 5?

Focus on Testing

You will hear two speakers. After each speaker finishes talking, you will hear a question. To answer the question, read the four possible answers and decide which one is the best answer. Circle the letter of the best answer.

SPEAKER 1

COLLEGE STUDENT: Wow, Frank! You mean you're taking French 4, Biology 2, Intro to Economics, American Civilization, Music Appreciation, *and* Beginning Acting! That's a really heavy load for your first semester of college.

Question: What is the speaker implying?

SPEAKER 2

COLLEGE STUDENT: I can't believe this! I'm spending over $2,000 a year for this meal plan, and it doesn't include meals on Saturday and Sunday!

Question: Why is the speaker unhappy?

CHAPTER three

Relationships

Family Networks and the Elderly, Part 1

PROFESSOR: Good morning. Good. We've got 12 people signed up for this seminar. This is the first time that the Sociology Department has offered an undergraduate seminar dealing with families and aging. I'm really glad to see so much interest in this topic.

Well, to begin. . . . This week and next I'm going to lecture on family networks and the elderly. I'm starting with this topic because I have decided to make this the focus of your class project. And I want you to have plenty of time to think, research, and plan your project presentations.

Today I'm going to define some terms and discuss some statistics on the family in the United States. Next week I'm going to present some cross-cultural data on the elderly from some research done quite some time ago—in the sixties. I haven't found any studies on this topic more recent than that. That's why I thought this would make a perfect research project for you. I would like you to work as a team to update this research for your class project. After I present what I've been able to find on this topic, we'll devise a research plan and divide up the work. Okay?

STUDENTS: Great. Sure. Sounds good.

PROFESSOR: Good. Let's look at some definitions of terms. First of all, the elderly. How old do you have to be to be considered elderly?

STUDENT 1: 75?

STUDENT 2: 65?

STUDENT 3: 70?

STUDENT 4: 55?

PROFESSOR: Well, the elderly are generally defined as people over sixty-five. Now let's look at two more definitions: nuclear family and extended family. Does anyone know the difference?

STUDENT 5: I learned in my anthro class last term that usually a nuclear family has a man, a woman, and their children.

PROFESSOR: That's right. By and large, the nuclear family consists of a husband, a wife, and children. However, if there are no children, then the husband and wife are the nuclear family. Of course, there may be only one parent due to a death, separation, or divorce. In this case, the nuclear family is the single parent and children. What about an extended family?

STUDENT 2: I think that's when you put two or more nuclear families together. Then you have an extended family.

PROFESSOR: That's right. For the most part, in an extended family a married couple is living with either the husband's parents or the wife's parents. But the couple may also live with aunts, uncles, cousins, and others who are not blood relations.

The extended family pattern is favored in some countries. For example, as a rule, people choose to live in extended families in Africa and Japan. In other countries, the nuclear family pattern is favored. In these countries, when people can choose the pattern they wish, they normally choose to live only with their nuclear family. This is true in the United States and Germany, for example.

Let's take a look at the United States and the nuclear family here. I'll tell you some interesting statistics about family patterns in the United States. These are statistics that are often reported in popular magazines or newspapers to show that family life in the United States is not very good. In fact, they make it seem like family life in the United States is so bad that there are hardly any families left. Let's look at these statistics.

1. Since the beginning of the twentieth century, there has been a decline in the average size of households and a dramatic increase in the percentage of one-person households.
2. Americans move a great deal. Believe it or not, 18% of American households moved last year.
3. Let's face it, today in the United States one in every two marriages ends in divorce. And
4. You may be surprised to find that over 60% of the children born in 1987 will spend some time in single-parent households by the time they are 18. That's nearly two out of every three children.

STUDENT 3: Gosh, I had no idea!

STUDENT 1: Yes, I *am* really surprised by this data!

PROFESSOR: These statistics indicate recent changes. Looking at these changes has led people to make some assumptions about the breakdown of family life and why the elderly have become alienated in the United States. Let's consider four of these assumptions, and then let's look at how true they are according to recent sociological research.

The first assumption based on these changes is that since Americans move a great deal, the elderly live at great distances from their children.

The second assumption is that the elderly are alienated from their children; therefore, the majority of the elderly do not see their children on a regular basis.

The third assumption is that because more Americans live in nuclear families than in extended families, the majority of old people rarely see their relatives, including their siblings. "Siblings" here means "brothers and sisters."

The fourth assumption deals with health. In the United States there are many offices and programs for helping the poor, the ill, and the elderly. Therefore, families no longer need to take care of old people, so they don't.

Well, that's enough to think about today. Next time, we'll look closely at these assumptions. We'll see if there's any data—any statistics—that can really support this thinking.

LECTURE *Family Networks and the Elderly, Part 2*

PROFESSOR: Well, let's see. Where were we? Where did we stop last time?

STUDENT 2: We were talking about the breakdown of family life in the United States.

STUDENT 4: And the assumptions people make about how this affects the elderly.

PROFESSOR: Right! We were talking about four assumptions people make about the breakdown of family life and the alienation of the elderly in the United States. Okay. Let's look at these assumptions again. Molly?

STUDENT 2: The first assumption, I think, based on these changes in family life, is that since Americans move a great deal, the elderly live mostly at great distances from their children.

PROFESSOR: Good, Molly. Han, give us another one.

STUDENT 5: You told us that people assume that the elderly are generally alienated from their children. And that, therefore, they also assume that a majority of the elderly don't see their children on a regular basis.

PROFESSOR: Exactly. You've either got a great memory or you take terrific notes!! Why are you laughing?

STUDENT 2: Well Han does have a great memory, but he also takes terrific notes. Most of us have gotten together with him this week to review our notes from our last class. He really helped us fill in some of the things we missed. It also helped to talk it through together.

PROFESSOR: Well, that's great. That's exactly the kind of teamwork you're going to need to complete the research project for this course. Okay, so who can give us another assumption that you reviewed together?

STUDENT 1: Is the third assumption that because more Americans live in nuclear families than in extended families, the majority of old people rarely see their siblings or other relatives?

PROFESSOR: Yes. And the fourth?

STUDENT 3: The fourth assumption deals with health. In the United States there are many offices and programs for helping the poor, the ill, and the elderly. People assume that since families no longer need to take care of old people, they don't.

PROFESSOR: Good work. Okay. . . . Now, let's look at these four beliefs—these assumptions—again and see just how true they are according to some research that was begun in the sixties. Let's see if the data—the statistics—from this research can support these assumptions. This research was done by Ethel Shanas at the University of Illinois, Chicago Circle.

Okay. Let's look at the first belief. The first belief is that children live very far from their parents due to the fact that Americans move so often. Let's see what percentage of the elderly live in the same household with their children, or live within ten minutes of their children. Let's see what Shanas found. In the United States, 60 percent of the elderly live with their children or within ten minutes of their children. Shanas's study also included some European countries. Look at your handout and you can see that more elderly people in the United States live with their children or within ten minutes of their children by car than in Denmark. However, it is interesting to note that most of the elderly people interviewed for another recent survey preferred to live in their own homes or apartments rather than with their children.

Now let's look at the second belief. This one says that old people are alienated from their children. Such a situation would mean that even though they may live close to their children, they do not see their children very often. Look at Table 2 on the handout. In Table 2 you can see that over 50 percent of the elderly had seen their children that day or the day before. In any case, over 78 percent of the elderly had seen their children within the last week. From the handout again you can see how the United States compares with the European countries studied.

Now let's look at the third belief: the belief that because the nuclear family is so strong, the elderly do not see their siblings (brothers and sisters) or other relatives. As you can see on the handout, this is not true either.

Finally, let's look at the belief that because there are offices and programs to take care of the elderly, families no longer care for old people in the United States. Medicare, a program to help the elderly with their medical bills, was passed into law in 1966. Many people expected that after the law was passed families would no longer take care of their elderly. But this didn't happen. Before the law was passed,

4 percent of the elderly were in institutions. After the law was passed, only 5 percent were in institutions. This is not a significant increase at all. In fact, most elderly people who live with their children are not in good health. They are living with their children because they are sick. If they were well, they would live on their own.

So now, let's reexamine what we have learned today about the elderly. First, the truth of the matter is that most older people do not live far from their children. In my opinion, this is one reason to be hopeful about the continuation of close-knit family life in the United States. Second, most of the elderly frequently see their children and also their siblings and other relatives. So it seems to me that the elderly are not alienated. Finally, we found out that the elderly are taken care of more often by their families than by public programs. So from my point of view, we can, in general, feel good about how the elderly are treated in the United States.

STUDENT 2: At least according to the statistics from Shanas' study in the sixties!

PROFESSOR: Yes, Molly. And that's why I thought it would be a good idea to do a pilot study for an update of Shanas' data. What do you think we'll find? Do you think things have changed in the last twenty to thirty years? Do you think these assumptions are still false, or might they be true now? Let's take a break, and then we'll begin to develop our research plan.

SKILL   *Introducing Information*

Conversations

Listen to the following conversations for examples of expressions used to introduce surprising information.

CONVERSATION 1

Mark tells Connie something surprising about his grandfather. Listen to the speakers and answer the question.

MARK: Hey, guess what!

CONNIE: What?

MARK: You won't believe this, but my grandfather called and said he's just joined an athletic club.

CONNIE: What's so surprising about that?

MARK: Well, he's eighty-five years old and has always hated sports and exercise of any kind as far as I know.

Question: Which expressions does Mark use to introduce the surprising information?

CONVERSATION 2

Uncle George and his niece, Gina, exchange some surprising information. Listen to the speakers and answer the question.

GEORGE: Surprise!

GINA: Uncle George, how nice to see you! Where's Aunt June? Isn't she with you?

GEORGE: Nope! Believe it or not, she decided to stay home this trip. She always liked the drive up here to see you kids, but I think her arthritis has been bothering her lately, so she decided to stay home.

GINA: Well, you may be surprised to know that I'm old enough to drive now, so maybe my brother and I can come down to visit her soon, okay?

GEORGE: Oh, I'm sure she'd love that!

Question: Which expressions do Uncle George and Gina use to introduce their surprises?

Focus on Testing

You will hear two speakers. After each speaker finishes talking, you will hear a question. To answer the question, read the four possible answers and decide which one is the best answer. Circle the letter of the best answer.

SPEAKER 1

MOTHER: O.K. kids, listen up. Normally we divide up the housework, but this week Dad has to give a big presentation at work. So, James and Ruth, you're both going to have to pitch in more around here.

Question: What is the speaker's main point?

SPEAKER 2

FATHER: We hardly ever take the dog on our summer vacation, but she's getting so old and looks so sad when we leave her. I can't bear to think of her in a kennel again. You think she'll like the Grand Canyon?

Question: What is the father trying to say to the family?

CHAPTER four

Health

What Makes Us Tick: The Cardiac Muscle

FRED: You know, getting together to study really helps me. I'm sure that's one reason I aced the last exam.

SUSAN: It helps me, too. Let's get going. I'm supposed to meet Charlie at the student union at 10:00.

FRED: Well, I'd say that's *one* way to study about the heart!

SUSAN: Oh no, we're just . . .

TORY: Never mind, you two. C'mon, relax. We'll be done by then, anyway. We've only got the stuff from Professor Miller's lecture to go over. And, boy! I found that stuff so interesting, I think I remember most of it already.

SUSAN: Yeah, me, too. And I'm now convinced that cardiac muscles are the most amazing muscles in the body. Let's see. What did Professor Miller say? That it's undoubtedly the action of these muscles that makes such a small organ as the heart so incredibly efficient?

TORY: Yup. That's right. Now, why don't we go through the notes and make sure we've gotten everything—okay?

SUSAN: Sure.

FRED: Great. Let me just get my notes out. Okay—go.

TORY: Well, first she talked about the shape of the heart.

FRED: It kind of reminds me of a pear.

SUSAN: Gosh, Fred, you're always thinking about food.

FRED: No—really. To my mind, it's just like a pear. Think of the pictures of the heart Professor Miller showed us. I'm positive it looked just like a pear, right side up, with the widest part at the bottom, just leaning a little to the right.

TORY: Yeah—I can imagine that. Now the parts: It's got four hollow chambers—two in the top part and two in the bottom part. Now what did she say about the walls of the heart?

FRED: She said that they're fairly thick at the bottom, about the thickness of a slice of bread, I guess. At the top, they're thinner. I'd say they're about the thickness of an orange peel.

SUSAN: There you go. See . . . always thinking about food. I told you.

FRED: Okay, okay. I'll think of some other analogies to help us learn this stuff. Now where was I? Oh—yeah. . . . The strips of heart muscle that wind around the bottom of the heart are like a string around a hollow ball. Is that better?

SUSAN & TORY: Yes, Yes. Go on. Great.

FRED: You know, I was surprised that the heart is so small. It's only slightly larger than a tightly-closed hand. I like how Professor Miller had us close our fists and look at them so we could see that they were about the same size as our hearts. Let's see. That's about five inches long and three and one-half inches wide. And the thickness is only two and a half inches. How much did she say the heart weighed?

TORY: It weighs between ten ounces and a pound. Then remember how she told us to open and close our hands. And to try to do it 75 times a minute. She was pretty sure our hands would get tired. Why don't we try it for half a minute.

SUSAN & FRED: Okay.

TORY: Ready? Go! Wow! My hand got really tired.

SUSAN: Thank goodness the heart doesn't. So . . . she wanted us to see how the muscles first contract and then relax, contract and relax, contract and relax—over and over again our whole lives.

FRED: Yup. That's the heartbeat. A rhythmic contraction and relaxation. Very regular and even, just like the tick tock of a clock.

SUSAN: But didn't she say that the rate can vary?

TORY: Yeah . . . In general, the rate of the heartbeat varies in relation to the size of the person or animal. An elephant's heart averages about 25 beats per minute. A canary's heart averages about 1,000 beats per minute. The heart of a human infant at birth beats about 130 times a minute. In a small child, it beats about 90 to 100 times a minute depending on the age and size of the child. The average adult rate for men is about 75 beats per minute. And the rate for women averages about 7 to 8 beats faster per minute than the rate for men. You think that's because women are smaller than men?

FRED: Nah . . . I suspect the heart generally just beats faster when you're in love. Right, Susan?

SUSAN: Fred . . . stop . . . I told you . . .

TORY: Okay. Okay. Anyway . . . this adds up to 100,000 heartbeats a day for an adult male, or about 2,600,000,000 heartbeats during a lifetime of seventy years. Let's see. What else?

SUSAN: Well, I still say that the cardiac muscle is undoubtedly the most amazing muscle in the body.

FRED: Why so?

SUSAN: Well, I find it pretty amazing that unlike the other muscles or organs the heart has no nerves in it. So, no messages are sent from the brain through nerves to the cardiac muscles. The brain doesn't tell the cardiac muscles to beat. Nothing does. The heartbeat starts in the cardiac muscle itself. It's the rhythmic quality of the cardiac muscle that keeps the heart beating and beating all of our lives. Remember what Professor Miller said about how in a laboratory, a very small piece of cardiac muscle can be kept alive in a dish with special liquid in it? And that the muscle will continue to beat all by itself!

FRED: Really?

SUSAN: Uh-huh. Scientists don't understand exactly the origin of the heartbeat yet, but I'm convinced that they will—in, say, 10 or 15 years.

FRED: Okay, but how does the heart work together with all of the other organs?

TORY: The heart's really like a pump, isn't it? It pumps blood to the rest of the body. Now let's see, I've got it here in my notes. The heart pumps approximately 5 quarts of blood a minute if you are resting and might pump up to 35 quarts of blood a minute if you are exercising—say swimming or playing tennis. You know, that means it may pump 4,500 gallons a day. It pumps 40,951,000 gallons (or 150,000,000 liters) of blood in a lifetime. The weight of this blood would be 150,000 tons. Wow! I'd say that the heart works incredibly hard, wouldn't you?

FRED: Don't look so worried, Tory. I don't think your heart is going to quit yet.

SUSAN: Right, Tory. Remember . . . Professor Miller said that the heart rests a lot, too. In fact, the heartbeat takes eight-tenths of a second, and half of that time the heart rests. I imagine that the heart rests because we can't take it to a body shop for repairs. But with the advances in modern medicine, I personally think that someday we'll be able to get heart repairs as easily as car repairs. Now, you may not agree with me, but I strongly believe that that day isn't far away. In fact, I suspect that by the year 2005 heart repairs will be almost as common as, as . . . uh, tooth repairs.

FRED: Well, you might be right, but. . . .

SUSAN: Oops . . . I gotta go meet Charlie. See you guys! Thanks!

FRED & TORY: Bye. See Ya. Say Hi to Charlie for us! See you in class.

SKILL B *Expressing Opinions*

Conversations

Listen to the following conversations in which two people express their opinions.

CONVERSATION 1

Here is a brief debate between Joe and Paul. Listen to the speakers and answer the questions.

JOE: I suspect that heart disease is the number one killer in the United States.

PAUL: No, no! It's cancer.

JOE: Well, I'm almost positive that it's heart disease. Didn't Dr. Strongheart say that . . .

PAUL: Nope. You're wrong. It's cancer.

Question 1: Does Joe express an opinion?

Question 2: Does Paul express an opinion?

Question 3: Does Paul indicate that his is a personal opinion?

Question 4: Which person sounds like a "know-it-all"? Why?

CONVERSATION 2

Let's give Joe and Paul another chance. Listen to the speakers and answer the question.

JOE: I suspect that heart disease is the number one killer in the United States.

PAUL: Oh, I always thought it was cancer.

JOE: Well, I'm almost positive that it's heart disease. Didn't Dr. Strongheart say that . . .

PAUL: Yes, but—not everyone will agree with me—I'm pretty sure Dr. Strongheart doesn't have his facts straight.

Question: What expressions does Paul use this time to introduce his personal opinions?

Focus on Testing

You will hear two speakers. After each speaker finishes talking, you will hear a question. To answer the question, read the four possible answers and decide which one is the best answer. Circle the letter of the best answer.

SPEAKER 1

MAN: Personally, I don't think that anyone should smoke and I'm positive that smoking causes cancer. Now not everyone will agree with me, but I don't think we should make laws about what people can and can't do in restaurants and bars.

Question: What is the speaker implying?

WOMAN: I bet I should lose some weight. I read in the newspaper that most Americans are eight to sixteen pounds overweight and I'm pretty sure that I'm part of this vast majority.

Question: What does the speaker think?

CHAPTER five

High Tech, Low Tech

<u>FIELD TRIP DEMONSTRATION</u>   *Space Flight: A Simulation*

GUIDE: Hello. We'd like to welcome Professor Chapman and his aeronautics class to Houston, Texas and the Lyndon B. Johnson Space Center. Today, without leaving the ground, we are going to experience the excitement and thrill of a flight into space.

We are now seated in the space center's amphitheater. The screen in front of you shows the inside of the space shuttle orbiter. The advanced technology used in this presentation will simulate for you, help you to sense, what it is like to be a crew member at work on an actual space mission. Our mission today is to capture and repair a 75 million dollar solar observation satellite that has been in orbit since 1980.

Okay. Fasten your seatbelts and we will begin our simulated flight aboard the spaceship *Enterprise*.

All right? Now, imagine we have been inside the orbiter for about two hours making sure everything is ready.

MISSION CONTROL: This is Mission Control. It is now T minus 3.8 seconds.

GUIDE: T stands for take-off, of course. And we hear the three engines of the orbiter fire.

MISSION CONTROL: T minus 1 second. T minus Zero.

GUIDE: At T minus zero the booster rockets on either side fire, and three seconds later we are lifted off the ground by the combined energy of the five engines.

Through the window we see the tower disappear from view. We feel the heavy effects of acceleration on our bodies as our spaceship builds up to four times the speed of sound (which is about eleven hundred feet per second in the air) and revolves one hundred and twenty degrees. Our antigravity suits keep us from getting sick. We are now turned with our heads toward the ground as we climb in the air and go out over the ocean. How do you like the feeling? We won't be right side up until we are in orbit.

Two minutes after takeoff the fuel in the booster rockets has been used up. They drop away as we continue gaining speed. Six minutes later we have reached fifteen times the speed of sound. Now the huge external tank drops away, and the graceful spaceship is flying free, heading into orbit around the earth at a height of 690 miles.

Once we reach full altitude we change our navigational computer program. This shuts down the main engines, and we can now control the shuttle's movement with small bursts of rocket fire from engines in the nose and tail. Put your hand on the control stick. Move the control stick to the right and we will roll. Although we don't feel it without gravity, you can see the motion through the window. If you move your wrist on the control forward or backward, we will go up and down. A twist makes us go to the right or left.

Let's have a few of you take turns with this, so you can get the full effect.

STUDENT 1: "My turn? OK. Here we go. Lean left!"

STUDENT 2: "OK, now I'll straighten us up."

STUDENT 3: "Anyone for a complete roll?"

ALL STUDENTS: Enough! Enough! I'm getting dizzy!

GUIDE: Okay. Let's get ready for the next phase of your mission.

Look through the window. The cargo doors are coming open. These doors open when we arrive in orbit and remain open to provide the ship with necessary ventilation throughout our stay in space. Our orders indicate that the purpose of this mission is to repair a $75 million solar observation satellite that has been in orbit since 1980. Since the failure of its control system, the satellite has been going through space without guidance—going so fast that it cannot be reached directly by the remote manipulation arm, which we'll call the RMA.

The RMA is a fifty-foot mechanical arm attached to the outside of the orbiter. Look at the handout we gave you as you came into the amphitheater. From the drawing, you can see that the mechanical arm is very much like your own arm. The arm is attached to the orbiter at the shoulder, and an "elbow" and a "wrist" allow the arm to move and bring satellites into the cargo bay of the orbiter. This is necessary in order to repair the satellite. There are television cameras at both the elbow and wrist so we can see what's going on. The "hand," or what is called the *end effector,* is fitted with three inside wires. A short arm of the satellite is caught by these wires.

If you look out the window, you will see two astronauts in spacesuits outside. They are about to manually slow down the satellite so that those of us inside the orbiter can connect it to the RMA. Remember, we said that the satellite was moving too quickly to be picked up directly by the RMA.

STUDENT 1: Wow, Look at that!

STUDENT 2: Yeah, they're actually grabbing that satellite with their hands!

GUIDE: Now it's our turn. The astronauts outside have captured the satellite for us and now we have to get to work. We must manipulate the controls for the arm, bending its wrist, elbow, and shoulder joints to lower the damaged satellite into our cargo bay.

Great job! Okay, now let's wait while the astronauts repair the satellite in the cargo bay. It should only take a few moments. Just a small part on the outside of it needs replacement. Uh, huh, they almost have the old part off. That's it. Now they're putting the new part in place. And tightening it down. There! I think they've got it!

MISSION CONTROL: Enterprise, this is Mission Control. Your mission has been accomplished. Congratulations! Have a good lunch. Then prepare for reentry.

GUIDE: Sorry crew, we'll have to skip lunch. No eating in the amphitheater, but you can sample some typical space shuttle meals in the cafeteria when you have completed the rest of your mission. Okay?

STUDENTS: "Sure." "Okay." "Great." "Fine."

GUIDE: Now we get ready for reentry by closing the cargo bay doors. We fire our engines to slow the shuttle so that it begins to deorbit, or fall toward earth. We enter the atmosphere at an altitude of 400,000 feet. We are now 5,000 miles from our landing site. The friction of air causes us to slow down from our entry speed of 16,000 miles per hour, but it also causes us to heat up. We are protected by the thermal tiles covering the ship from surface temperatures of 2,750 degrees Fahrenheit. The heat is so great that our radio communications are blocked for twelve minutes on our descent. Our on-board computers maintain control.

As the atmosphere thickens, our craft changes from a spaceship into a glider. The jets shut off as we continue our descent in silence. The ground is coming up at us alarmingly fast at 10,000 feet per minute, seven times faster than it would in the landing of an airplane. At just 1,500 feet our stomachs feel funny as the pilot pulls up the nose of the spaceship to slow us down. We hear the landing gear open and lock, and before we can experience another moment's fear and exhilaration, we touch back down on Mother Earth and come to a stop.

The flight is over. Mission accomplished! Thanks for coming aboard the *Enterprise*. See you next time on our sister ship *Discovery*.

SKILL B **Shifting Focus**

Conversations

In the following four conversations, you will hear the active voice contrasted with the passive voice, and the personal with the impersonal. Listen to the conversations and answer the questions after conversations 2 and 4.

CONVERSATION 1

A mother and father are standing in the front yard talking.

MOTHER: Why is the baby crying?
FATHER: I don't know, but a dog just ran out of the yard.
MOTHER: There are teeth marks on her arm!
FATHER: Oh, no! The dog must have bitten her!

CONVERSATION 2

Two police officers are talking to each other.

POLICE OFFICER 1: What was that last phone call about?
POLICE OFFICER 2: The mother of a small baby was really upset and she wants us to find a stray dog.
POLICE OFFICER 1: Why? Was there any trouble?
POLICE OFFICER 2: Yes, the baby was bitten by the dog.

Question 1: Which conversation (1 or 2) contains the passive voice?
Question 2: Why do you think the passive voice was used in this situation?

CONVERSATION 3

A husband and wife are in the living room talking.

HUSBAND: What happened?
WIFE: The lights just went out!
HUSBAND: What do you suppose is the reason?
WIFE: They probably turned off our electricity because we didn't pay our bill!

CONVERSATION 4

A woman is on the phone with an electric company employee.

ELECTRIC COMPANY OFFICIAL: Good morning. This is Madison Electric.
CUSTOMER: My name is Ellen Bates and my electricity went out last night.
ELECTRIC COMPANY OFFICIAL: Just a minute, Mrs. Bates. I'll check your records.
CUSTOMER: Thank you.
ELECTRIC COMPANY OFFICIAL: Ah, yes, here they are.
CUSTOMER: What happened?
ELECTRIC COMPANY OFFICIAL: Your electricity has been turned off because your bill hasn't been paid.

Question 1: Which conversation (3 or 4) contains the passive voice?
Question 2: Why do you think the passive voice was used in this situation?

Focus on Testing

You will hear two speakers. After each speaker finishes talking, you will hear a question. To answer the question, read the four possible answers and decide which one is the best answer. Circle the letter of the best answer.

SPEAKER 1

WOMAN: Yeah, the airport was hit, too. The Weather Service says that all flights have been canceled until further notice.

Question: What has happened at the airport?

SPEAKER 2

MAN: Due to technical difficulties the shuttle lift-off for today has been canceled. We'll let you know when repairs are completed and it's been rescheduled.

Question: What is the speaker explaining?

CHAPTER SIX

Money Matters

MICHELLE BARNEY: Good afternoon. This is Radio K-I-Z-Z, your "total talk" radio station with another edition of *The World at Large.* I am Michelle Barney, Radio K-I-Z-Z financial reporter, and I will be your host for today's program, "The World Bank Under Fire."

About three-quarters of the world's population lives in developing countries. Until recently, a developing country was generally understood to be one that was not yet highly industrialized. It was usually located in Africa, Asia, or Latin America. Lately, however, with the fall of communism in Eastern Europe and the break-up of the Soviet bloc nations, semi-industrialized countries that are struggling to survive as they build new economic systems have also been placed in the developing nation category. What all developing countries have in common is that the people of these countries do not have enough money to invest in such things as schools, utilities, factories, and highways. One way these countries can get money is by borrowing money from an organization called the World Bank.

As of June, 1993, the World Bank held $140 billion dollars in loans to poor nations. In theory, this huge sum of money should be helping the world's poor. Since the establishment of the World Bank in 1944, most people have assumed that these loans could only do good things for a country. But it turns out that money isn't everything.

For example, many people are now questioning the value of a dam being built with World Bank money in India. That dam will displace, make homeless, more people than it would eventually serve with electric power, and it will also destroy scarce forestlands as well as endangered animals and plants. Also being questioned are loans for projects that are not supported by government policies. For example, irrigation projects to raise farm production won't make more money for a country if the government of that country keeps food prices too low.

Today we have a spokesperson from the World Bank, Mr. George Cruz, here with us in the studio. Mr. Cruz has been with the bank for ten years and is part of a high-level internal bank team that has been examining the effectiveness of World Bank projects. It seems that this team of insiders is coming to the same conclusions that many critics of the World Bank have come to: that many of the projects are economic failures and that the environmental and human rights issues are so serious that the United States and other industrialized countries are being pressured to stop contributing money to World Bank projects. Mr. Cruz. . . .

GEORGE CRUZ: Well, Ms. Barney, I am very happy to be here today to clarify some things about the World Bank. While much of what you say is true, I think it needs to be put into a larger context, which includes the successes of the World Bank as well as the failures, if you will.

If I may, I'd like to start with a brief overview of the World Bank and how it works.

MS. BARNEY: Of course. I think that would be very helpful for our listeners.

MR. CRUZ: Now, what we call the World Bank is actually the umbrella term, the general term, for three separate organizations with three slightly different purposes. First, there's the International Bank for Reconstruction and Development. This is the organization most people have in mind when they think of the World Bank. In order to borrow money from this branch of the World Bank, a country must be a member. It's sort of like joining a club, but instead of paying an initiation fee, instead of paying money to join the club, the club lends you money (although the money is supposed to be paid back with interest, as with any bank loan).

MS. BARNEY: Yes. But isn't it true that many countries have been defaulting on the loans. I'm not talking about the amount of the loan itself. They're not even paying the interest on the loans!

MR. CRUZ: Yes, that has been an issue in the past, but we have started a program to restructure the loans which will alleviate that problem.

Where was I? Oh, yes. The International Bank for Reconstruction and Development loans money to member countries for projects that will aid economic development. In theory, this is good. *But* this bank can only loan money to buy imported goods. And to make sure that this rule is followed, the bank pays the sellers directly.

MS. BARNEY: Well, this is good for the countries that want to sell goods to developing countries, but wouldn't this discourage local production of goods? In the long run, wouldn't this do more harm than good to the developing country's economy?

MR. CRUZ: Possibly. That's one of the things we're trying to look at. But there are other advantages to getting a loan from this arm of the World Bank. The International Bank for Reconstruction and Development provides technical assistance as well as loans.

For example, Cameroon applied for a loan for a new irrigation system along the Logone River. They hoped that with this new irrigation system the cash income of the region would be five times greater than before. But the Bank did not approve the project right away. Because we know that technological advances can sometimes cause environmental problems, before approving the project, the Bank asked environmental consultants to prepare an environmental impact report.

The consultants found that the new irrigation system would result in a serious health problem. This was because of the snails that live in the area. These snails carry a tropical disease called bilharzia.

MS. BARNEY: Excuse me. Was that bil*har*zia with an "h"?

MR. CRUZ: Yes. Bil-har-zee-uh. Bilharzia. Anyway, the snails posed a serious health problem, and the new irrigation system might spread the snails and the disease they carried to a larger area.

So the Bank paid for studies of the river system. Scientists and engineers working together determined that if the irrigation system was used when the snails were not breeding, then the disease would not spread. So, the Bank was able to find a solution to the problem.

MS. BARNEY: Yes, I read about that project. But wasn't there a problem getting the local residents to use the system appropriately once it was completed. I believe I read that some people could never be convinced that the problem, the "snail disease scare," had really been taken care of, so they would not use the irrigation system at all. And that another large group of people never believed there was a problem in the first place, so they would not stop using the irrigation system when the snails were breeding.

MR. CRUZ: Yes, that's quite true. The International Bank for Reconstruction and Development is beginning to see that an understanding of the local culture and needs may be more important than anything else for the success of a project.

Well, let me continue. The second organization under the World Bank umbrella is the International Development Association, or IDA. The IDA has approximately 160 members and makes loans that are interest free. This, of course, is good for needy countries. It allows even the poorest country to begin projects immediately, without having to worry about interest payments. On the other hand, because little or no interest is paid, the IDA is very dependent upon contributions from member nations to support various projects.

MS. BARNEY: Yes, and this is where contributing nations could attach some strings to the loans, right? This is how the superpowers can begin to dictate what sort of governmental policies must be in place before loans will be given.

MR. CRUZ: Yes, exactly. But it remains to be seen whether this is a good or a bad thing, I think.

So, let's move on to the third organization in the World Bank group: The International Finance Corporation, or IFC. The IFC is different from the International Bank for Reconstruction and Development or the IDA because the IFC can invest in private business and industry, while the other two organizations can only invest in government projects. This is good for the country because the government does not have to guarantee the loan and it encourages the growth of private business or industry. On the other hand, the IFC is not protected if the business fails.

Also, the IFC has no control over how a company spends its money. But some people might say that the best loans have no strings attached, right?

MS. BARNEY: Absolutely, but is that ever really possible? I mean, borrowing money from the IFC, with absolutely no strings attached? I thought that the member nations get voting rights based on the amount of money they contribute to the Bank. Doesn't that mean that the wealthier nations have the greatest influence on how and to whom the money will be given—that is, which projects will be financed?

MR. CRUZ: Ideally, of course, the loans are made to countries on the basis of economic need alone. But, we all know that it is difficult to separate economic goals and political interests in today's world.

Robert McNamara, who was secretary of defense when John F. Kennedy was president of the United States, was president of the World Bank for a time. He hoped that the World Bank would be a model of international cooperation free from political self-interests. He envisioned a world in which the superpowers would join together in providing financial support for developing nations instead of quarreling among themselves.

MS. BARNEY: Yes, that is a wonderful idea. But whether the World Bank can ever fulfill this promise remains to be seen.

Well, our time is up and that brings us to the end of this week's edition of *The World at Large*. Our guest today was George Cruz and the topic was "The World Bank Under Fire." Thank you for being with us today, Mr. Cruz.

MR. CRUZ: My pleasure.

MS. BARNEY: Well, this is Michelle Barney, your host for *The World at Large*. Please join us next week, same time, same station, K-I-Z-Z, your total talk radio.

SKILL B   *Agreeing and Disagreeing*

Conversations

Listen to the following conversations in which expressions of agreement and disagreement are used both correctly and incorrectly.

CONVERSATION 1

In a college classroom, a student is challenging an instructor. Listen to the speakers and answer the questions.

INSTRUCTOR: And furthermore, it is my contention that had it not been for aid from neighboring countries, the war would have been lost.

STUDENT: You've got to be kidding! Military planning was the key.

Questions: Do you think the student is being polite or rude? Why?

CONVERSATION 2

Now listen to another student respond to the same instructor and answer the questions.

INSTRUCTOR: And furthermore, it is my contention that if it wasn't for aid from neighboring countries, the war would have been lost.

STUDENT: Yes, but isn't it also true that excellent military planning helped?

Questions: Do you think this student responded appropriately? Why?

CONVERSATION 3

Two students are chatting in the school cafeteria. Listen to the speakers and answer the question.

ROGER: Hey, Paul. Looks like we're having corned beef hash again! The only time we have anything decent to eat is when the parents visit!

PAUL: Yes, Roger. That's precisely the point.

Question: Paul probably doesn't have too many friends. Why do you think this might be?

CONVERSATION 4

Let's give Paul another chance to respond to Roger a bit more appropriately. Listen, and then answer the question.

ROGER: Hey, Paul. Looks like we're having corned beef hash again! The only time we have anything decent to eat is when the parents visit!

PAUL: You can say that again, Roger.

Question: Why is the expression that Paul uses this time to agree with Roger much more appropriate?

CONVERSATION 5

At a corporation meeting, two board members are discussing future plans. Listen to the speakers and answer the questions.

BOARD MEMBER 1: It's obvious that if we don't branch out and get into other areas of interest, eventually the company will fail.

BOARD MEMBER 2: I don't believe that! We must cut costs!

Questions: Do you think that these board members will reach consensus easily? Why or why not?

CONVERSATION 6

Now listen to two other board members in a similar conversation. Answer the questions.

BOARD MEMBER 3: It's obvious that if we don't branch out and get into other areas of interest, eventually the company will fail.

BOARD MEMBER 4: That's more or less true; however, I think that by cutting our costs we can accomplish a great deal.

Question 1: Do you think these board members will be able to reach an agreement more or less easily than the board members in the previous conversation?

Question 2: How is this conversation different from the previous one?

CONVERSATION 7

At the doctor's office, a doctor and her patient's wife are discussing the patient. Listen to the speakers and answer the questions.

DOCTOR: Mrs. Franklin, your husband has a variety of medical problems and it's absolutely essential that he get more exercise.

MRS. FRANKLIN: I knew it! He's too fat!

Question 1: Is Mrs. Franklin, the patient's wife, agreeing or disagreeing with the doctor?

Question 2: Is Mrs. Franklin responding formally or informally?

CONVERSATION 8

Listen to the doctor and Mrs. Franklin again. This time Mrs. Franklin responds differently. Answer the questions.

DOCTOR: Mrs. Franklin, your husband has a variety of medical problems and it's absolutely essential that he get more exercise.

MRS. FRANKLIN: I couldn't agree with you more, Dr. Lewis. I've been trying to get him to diet for years.

Question 1: Is Mrs. Franklin responding formally or informally?

Question 2: Which of the two responses do you think is more appropriate and why?

Focus on Testing

You will hear two speakers. After each speaker finishes talking, you will hear a question. To answer the question, read the four possible answers and decide which one is the best answer. Circle the letter of the best answer.

SPEAKER 1

WOMAN: It's nice that banks are beginning to make more loans to poor people. On the other hand, that money comes with a lot of strings attached.

Question: What is the speaker implying?

SPEAKER 2

MAN: You can say that again! I couldn't agree with you more. It's definitely better to pay cash than to pay interest for years and years.

Question: What is the speaker implying?

CHAPTER seven

Leisure Time

Leisure Time in Our Society

LYNN MERIWEATHER: Hello, I'm Lynn Meriweather, President of the City Series Club, and I'd like to welcome all of you here today. I am pleased to introduce Professor Paulson, our guest speaker. Professor Paulson is a noted sociologist who specializes in how people use their leisure time. He has written many books on this subject and has given lectures all over the world, including Tokyo University and the London School of Economics. At the end of his talk, there will be time for questions. Please write your questions on the cards provided and pass them up to the front of the auditorium. The title of his talk is "Leisure Time in Our Society." Welcome, Professor Paulson.

PROFESSOR PAULSON: Thank you Ms. Meriweather. I'm very pleased to be here today and to be a part of your respected lecture series. Before we begin an analysis of the ways we spend our leisure time in today's society, I would like to fill you in on a bit of the history of leisure time. I will talk first about the history of leisure time because I think this historical perspective will help us understand present-day attitudes and trends a little better.

Did you know that the notion of "time off" is a product of modern industrial society, in other words, the Industrial Age? Yes, with industrialization came factories, and all the factories had time clocks. It was the workers punching time clocks in factories who made us so aware of "time on" the job and "time off" the job. Workers became concerned about how much of their time belonged to the factory owners and how much of it belonged to themselves.

In nonindustrialized or more agrarian societies, the division between time on and time off is not as clear. There are, of course, no time clocks on the farm. But even there you'll find plenty of days set aside for celebration, feasting, and rest.

Long ago, in prehistoric times—before written records of events were kept—we think there was probably little distinction or even no distinction between work and play, between time on and time off. How do you like that idea? People got up in the morning, gathered food, ate, then rested so that they could get up the next day, gather more food, eat, rest, and then continue this pattern day after day. To work was to live. I would have enjoyed living then; what about you? Do you think this pattern has changed?

Well, eventually, as human societies evolved, people began to farm the land. Some people became workers, and others became leaders, supervising the work. Ancient peoples were also eager to set aside time for play. The Roman calendar, for example, listed as many as 175 holidays per year at one point in the fifth century. That's about half the year. That sounds great to me. Does that appeal to you, too?

You may have noticed that we Americans in particular are possessive, and fiercely so, of our leisure time. This is not so surprising when you remember that the United States was founded as a democracy. That meant that the common worker should be able to participate in pleasures that were formerly only allowed the aristocracy, the royalty, and upper classes. This, of course, eventually led to scheduled time off or extended periods away from work. It seems that the "pursuit of happiness"—the inalienable right decreed in our Declaration of Independence from Great Britain in 1776—has come to mean "the pursuit of time off."

So the idea of leisure time—of taking time off—is not really a new one, but it seems to be relatively new for the common worker. The 175 Roman holidays I mentioned were probably meant only for the aristocracy, the upper classes. Slaves and common laborers had much less leisure time, but perhaps just a little bit less than workers do today. Does this surprise you? I'm not advocating slavery, however. I would still abhor being a slave no matter how much leisure time I had, wouldn't you?

It seems that we may be more concerned with our right to leisure time and we may pursue it more aggressively than people did in the past. But are we really working less and getting more leisure time now? Or does it only seem so?

We would like to believe that our 40-hour work week with a 2-week paid vacation is the shortest amount of working time per year ever achieved by a productive society. Yet, if we make a statistical comparison of time spent working in past ages with time spent working in our present society, we can see that this is not necessarily true.

Our 40-hour work week translates into about a 2,000-hour work year, about the same amount of time that Roman citizens worked in the middle of the fourth century. This work year, of course, did not apply to slaves and women, who were not considered citizens.

Craftsmen in France in the thirteenth century worked according to an elaborate set of rules established by their guilds, the medieval equivalent of trade unions. They were provided with a lunch hour, rest times, and rules limiting the amount of work to be done on Sunday or at night. Some craftsmen in Paris, for example, received 30 days of vacation in addition to the normal 141 days off per year. So in the end, most of these skilled workers put in between 2,000 and 2,500 hours per year. This is not much different from the amount of time most of us work today.

So, what happened? Why does it seem that we've achieved so much time off when perhaps we really haven't? Well, the work week of the common worker began to increase along with the growth of the Industrial Age. By 1750, a work week of 72 hours was usual in France and England. This trend reached its peak in the mid-nineteenth century, particularly in the highly mechanized textile industry, where even 14- to 18-hour workdays were not uncommon.

When we compare our present work week and vacation time to these statistics, we seem to have come a long way. But what, in fact, have we achieved, and at what cost? We've reduced the work week in industrialized countries to the same length enjoyed by workers in past ages. Not so much gained there! But workers today are more affluent—have more money to spend—than workers have ever had before. And the term "worker" includes many more categories than ever before. In medieval times the word worker referred mainly to clerical workers and skilled craftsmen and excluded common laborers and women. The word worker today includes all categories of people in the work force, skilled and unskilled, women and men. So any benefits for workers today actually apply to a much larger group of people than in past times. In other words, I'm happy to say more people have leisure time to spend than ever before, even though the amount of time per person may not have increased much. Well, I may have raised more questions than I've answered with this information. So I'd be happy to take a few questions now.

MS. MERIWEATHER: Thank you Professor Paulson. We do have a bit of time for questions from the audience. The first question is, "How important is culture in determining how we spend our holidays?"

PROFESSOR PAULSON: Oh, very important. In fact, we may have lost cultural cues about how to best use our leisure time. In other words, our free time, our time off, has become secularized. That is, it is no longer associated with religious observances. If a holiday were always a "holy day"—a day associated with religious traditions—we would have some cultural clue about what to do on this day. We would probably spend at least some part of it in worship—in prayer—in a church or temple or at home. But now our holidays are more likely to be named after presidents than saints, and recently labor unions have been suggesting that each worker's birthday should be considered a holiday for that worker. I love that idea, don't you? Anyone want to take the day off tomorrow to celebrate my birthday?

MS. MERIWEATHER: Professor Paulson, another member of our audience asks, "What do you think about Juliet Schor's book, *The Overworked American*? She says that the average worker today works about 163 hours more a year than their counterparts in the late 1960s."

PROFESSOR PAULSON: I've read Ms. Schor's book and she makes many good points. But most of the increase in work time is among women, who were not working as much in the sixties. And Thomas Juster and Frank Stafford at the University of Michigan as well as John Robinson of the University of Maryland have shown that the amount of leisure time has also risen since 1965.

MS. MERIWEATHER: Professor, we have time for one final question. "What recommendations do you have for how we should spend our leisure time?"

PROFESSOR PAULSON: Well, I think we must learn to give our free time meaning. We must continue to be creative in our leisure time as well as our work time in order to give our leisure time a purpose—and a significant place in our development as individuals and as a society.

MS. MERIWEATHER: Thank you so much for joining us today, Professor Paulson. And thank you to our audience. We hope to see you all at our next City Series lecture.

SKILL B   *Expressing Likes and Dislikes*

Conversations

Listen to the taped conversations. They demonstrate a wide variety of ways to express likes and dislikes.

CONVERSATION 1

A man is being interviewed for a job. Listen to the speakers and answer the questions.

INTERVIEWER: I'm happy to say we have quite a good recreation program for the employees.

APPLICANT: Now this is my idea of a job!

INTERVIEWER: Ah . . . yes . . . , well, we have a gym with exercise equipment to use before and after work or during the lunch hour.

APPLICANT: I can't stand that kind of exercise!

INTERVIEWER: Oh?

Questions: Do you think the man will get the job? Why or why not?

CONVERSATION 2

A woman is being interviewed for a job. Listen to the speakers and answer the questions.

INTERVIEWER: I'm delighted that you're interested in the company recreation program.

APPLICANT: Oh, yes. I really enjoy getting to know my co-workers in more informal circumstances.

INTERVIEWER: Well, we have a bowling team that gets together every Friday evening.

APPLICANT: I don't really care for bowling. Are there any other sports that the employees do as a group?

INTERVIEWER: How about softball—or bicycling?

APPLICANT: Yes, I enjoy bicycling. That would be nice.

Questions: Do you think the woman will get the job? Why or why not?

CONVERSATION 3

Rafael and Ana are discussing what to do with their leisure time. Listen to the speakers and answer the questions.

RAFAEL: Hey, want to go to the rock concert with me on Saturday?

ANA: Oh, no . . . I hate that kind of music.

RAFAEL: Oh, well, I thought you might like it.

ANA: No, I don't have time for that sort of thing.

Question 1: Does Ana enjoy rock concerts?

Question 2: Does she express her opinion strongly, or does she soften it?

Question 3: Do you think Rafael will ask Ana out again? Why or why not?

CONVERSATION 4

Rafael and Joyce are discussing what to do with their leisure time. Listen to the speakers and answer the questions.

RAFAEL: Hi! How about going to see that new play at the experimental theater tonight?

JOYCE: Thanks, but I don't especially like that type of theater.

RAFAEL: Oh, gee, I thought you would.

JOYCE: No, I dislike it because I don't usually understand what's happening.

Question 1: Does Joyce enjoy experimental theater?

Question 2: Does she express her opinion strongly?

Question 3: Do you think Rafael will ask Joyce out again? Why or why not?

Focus on Testing

You will hear two speakers. After each speaker finishes talking, you will hear a question. To answer the question, read the four possible answers and decide which one is the best answer. Circle the letter of the best answer.

SPEAKER 1

MAN: I just don't have time for garage sales! What a rotten way to spend a perfectly good Sunday—looking at other people's junk. How ridiculous.

Question: What does the speaker think?

SPEAKER 2

WOMAN: I really enjoy pot luck dinners. And I love chocolate. What a great idea—an all chocolate dessert pot luck. Now that's my idea of a great meal!

Question: What does the speaker think?

CHAPTER eight

Creativity

LECTURE

Creativity: As Essential to the Engineer as to the Artist

PROFESSOR: Today we will continue our discussion of the creative process in general and then take up the topic of what things might inhibit this process in your work as engineers. The material under discussion should be applicable to the area of specialization you have chosen: mechanical engineering, environmental engineering, electrical, industrial, civil—whatever.

Well—to pick up where we left off last time—I believe we agreed that creativity is a mysterious idea. It is one of those things we all recognize when we see it, but we do not really understand what it is. We seem to feel that some people are naturally creative, but we don't know how they got that way. Is creativity an inborn gift like athletic ability or good looks, or is it something that can be acquired, like money or knowledge? Perhaps if we analyze the creative process carefully, we might get some insight into what it is and how it might work in our lives.

The creative process has always been accepted as the source of all important work in the arts. But we should not think that creativity plays a role only in the arts. Every major scientific discovery began with someone imagining the world to look differently from the way others saw it. And this is what creativity is all about— imagining the world in a new way. And despite what you may believe about the limits of your own creative imaginations, we all have the potential to imagine the world in an absolutely new way. In fact, you're born with it. It is your birthright as a human being. Cave painters in the Stone Age had it. Musicians in the last century had it. And you have it. And, what's more, you use it every day, almost every moment of your life. Your creative imagination is what you use to make sense of your experiences. It is your creative mind that gets meaning from the chaos of your experiences and brings order to your world.

Let me emphasize again that (1) everyone has creative potential and (2) we are all creating our own realities at every moment. Let me illustrate this by having you look at the large No Smoking signs on the walls. Do you recognize the sign at one glance, or do you see it in parts, small sections, letter by letter? When I look hard and concentrate—that is, when I am deliberately analytical—I feel I see the world in pieces. That's because the eye, as you may know, really does "see" things in that way. But what is really going on is that the eye vibrates with great speed, taking brief, narrow pictures of the world. Then the mind combines or fuses those individual pictures into a larger picture—a creation. It's this creation that gives us a sense of the whole. So the mind, then, creates an interpretation of what comes in through the senses.

Now I'll explain how art is connected with this process of interpretation and ordering of the world. The artist sees a fragmentary, disordered series of events— pieces of light, color, moments in life, of conversation—and weaves them into a whole cloth to make the world understandable. Thus, the artist creates, as the poet Robert Frost said, ". . . a momentary stay against the confusion of the world." But art is not just an activity for professional artists. The real story is that we do the same things as the artist every day, at all times. We have been doing it since childhood and will continue to do it until we die. In this way, we are artists and creators in our lives, without effort.

Now you may be wondering at this point why so many people want to be more creative if, as we said, human beings are naturally creative all the time. I'm going to answer that by telling you about one of life's dirty tricks. It seems that although the mind is spontaneously creative when we are very young, as we grow older the mind tends to become caught in repetitive grooves or ruts. Then the mind operates imitatively—not creatively—seeing the world the same way day after day after day. In this state of mind nothing new can be developed because no new ways of looking at things are ever explored.

So the problem seems to be how to remove the barriers to creativity that we acquire as we grow older. We don't need to add something to ourselves that isn't already there, but we do need to find ways to free the creative potential that we already possess. To give a practical illustration of what I mean, I'd like to talk about something that I think often inhibits the creative process in people in our profession: our tendency to put too many limits on solutions to a problem. What do I mean by too many limits? Look at your handout. There you see nine dots in three rows. Try to draw no more than four straight lines that will touch all nine dots.

Did you solve the problem? You probably had trouble if you were not willing to go outside the imaginary limits enclosing the nine dots. Those boundaries are imaginary. Look at this solution.

STUDENTS: Wow! I'd never think of that! You've gotta be kidding! It seems so easy now! I got it! Yes! I got it!

PROFESSOR: Great! I'm glad some of you got it this way, but there are other solutions, too. Did any of you solve the puzzle in another way. Come on! Don't be shy! No idea is silly as long as it solves the problem. Yes, do you have a solution?

STUDENT 1: Well, you didn't say we had to use only a pen or pencil. So, I cut the dots apart and arranged them in a straight line and then connected them.

PROFESSOR: Very clever! Anyone else? Any other solutions? Yes, go ahead.

STUDENT 2: How about this: You can tape the handout of the puzzle to a globe and then keep circumnavigating the globe with your pen until you pass through all the dots.

PROFESSOR: Wonderful! Very imaginative! Now I have to tell you the solution that my ten-year-old daughter came up with. She solved the problem by using a veeeeery faaaat line! Okay. So now you see how your own mind may impose limits on the possible solutions to a problem because you're just seeing things in standard, ordinary ways. To be creative, we have to be able to look at things in extraordinary, new ways.

Obviously, when you try to solve a problem creatively, you have to figure out just what the problem is first. But don't state the problem too narrowly, too specifically, or you might limit the number of solutions that you will come up with. Let me give you another practical example of solving a problem creatively. Say your problem is to design a playground. If you consider the problem as one of putting the playground equipment in a certain space, you are looking at the problem too narrowly. If you think of it as a problem in both designing the playground equipment itself and then placing the equipment, well, you have given yourself a much more creative problem with a greater possibility for a variety of solutions. So I can't emphasize this enough: When you state a problem, don't state it too narrowly or you will see it too narrowly and you will limit the possible solutions.

So, you can see now how our creative potential can be blocked in a variety of ways. I have already mentioned two ways in which we each can do this to ourselves. But the real story is that our culture plays a big part in blocking creative potential. Psychologists say that people here in the United States and Canada seem to have four main cultural blocks to creativity. Let me list them for you. First, we tend to believe that fantasy, playfulness, and humor in problem solving are for children, not adults. Second, we tend to think that feelings, intuitions, and pleasure are bad, whereas logic, reason, and numbers are good. Third, most of us think that tradition is better than change. And finally, we believe that scientific thinking and great quantities of money can solve any problem.

Let's go over each of these in turn. First, despite what you may believe, humor and creativity are definitely linked. They both open up areas of thought and feeling and connect things or ideas that were never put together before. For example, with a joke—well, wait—let me illustrate. A psychiatrist and a patient are talking and the patient says, "I'm getting really worried about my brother, Doc. He thinks he's a chicken." And the doctor says, "Well, why don't you bring him to me for help?" And the patient answers, "Oh, no. We can't do that." "Why not?" asks the doctor. And the patient answers, "Because we need the eggs."

OK, OK. It's not a great joke, but think about it. You did laugh, so what has happened here? You expect that there will be logic to the story and the logic is broken by the surprise punch line. That's just what makes it work. The punch line about the eggs was not expected. Creativity is also the appearance of the unexpected. And by the way, there's another tie between humor and creativity. To be creative, you must be willing to be laughed at because we often laugh at the unusual. In fact, many of the important ideas in science were laughed at when they were first presented to the public.

OK, so the next item on our list of cultural blocks to creativity is that reason and logic are better than feelings and intuition. Now, while reason and logic are useful, many great ideas come to people while they are dreaming. In fact, one of the most famous works of the composer Richard Wagner came to him in a dream. So be open to your dreams, fantasies, and feelings.

The third thing to consider is tradition versus change. While tradition is valued and worthwhile, it is often a block to creativity because it represents the ordinary and familiar. The creative process, as we have said, involves things that are new and different. But this is not easy. Change takes hard work and often great courage. Working for change demands creativity.

And what do you think about the final point—that scientific thinking and great quantities of money can solve any problem? Yes, in the back, what do you think?

STUDENT 3: Well, I believe that this is true only when scientific thinking is also creative thinking. You know—in the ways you've been telling us about. I also think that the money itself has to be used creatively.

PROFESSOR: Yes, very interesting. We'll have to discuss that further when we've got more time.

So, in conclusion, I will summarize what I have been saying today and in previous lectures. The creative process cannot be observed. It is carried out unconsciously. But even though it is done unconsciously, the reality is that we can still train ourselves to be more creative people. We can do this by removing the limitations we place on ourselves and by becoming aware of any cultural blocks that may inhibit the creative process.

Well, that's all for today. Thank you, and see you next week.

Divulging Information

Conversations

Listen to these conversations, which present examples of ways to divulge information.

CONVERSATION 1

Albert and Bonnie are discussing the real reason that Professor Finster was fired. Listen to the speakers and answer the questions.

ALBERT: Did you hear that Professor Finster resigned from his post as president of the Institute of Reverse Psychology?
BONNIE: Yeah. I heard that story too.
ALBERT: Why do you say it's a story?
BONNIE: Because I've heard what's really going on. The fact of the matter is that he was forced to quit—fired, in fact.
ALBERT: No kidding—why?
BONNIE: Despite what you believe about him, he doesn't do very careful research and publishes inaccurate data.

Question 1: In this conversation formal or informal?
Question 2: What phrase helped you decide this?

CONVERSATION 2

Kate and Doug are discussing where Jules got the cash for his new motorcycle. Listen to the speakers and answer the questions.

KATE: Hey, what gives? That's a really fine motorcycle Jules is riding. Where'd he get the cash?
DOUG: I don't know.
KATE: Oh, come on—what's the scoop?
DOUG: Well, he says he saved up for it, but the real story is: He won the money gambling in Las Vegas and he doesn't want his folks to find out.
KATE: I thought he told Susie that he couldn't stand Las Vegas.
DOUG: Well, despite what you may have heard, the real story is that he's been sneaking off to Las Vegas just about every other weekend.

Question 1: Is this conversation formal or informal?
Question 2: What phrase helped you decide this?

Focus on Testing

You will hear two speakers. After each speaker finishes talking, you will hear a question. To answer the question, read the four possible answers and decide which one is the best answer. Circle the letter of the best answer.

SPEAKER 1

WOMAN: Let me illustrate my point about creativity. Grandma Moses never had an art lesson in her life and yet her paintings are displayed in art galleries.

Question: What is the speaker implying?

SPEAKER 2

MAN: I really can't emphasize this enough. Creativity is not sex or age linked.

Question: What is the speaker saying?

CHAPTER nine

Human Behavior

Group Dynamics

PROFESSOR: This afternoon I'm going to talk to you about a topic that affects every person in this room: group dynamics. Every person in this room is part of some group, right? At the very least, you belong to this class, a class of Social Psychology 1 students here at Jefferson College. But my guess is that you belong to other groups too, don't you? Your family, right? Your church? A social club perhaps? A soccer, golf, or tennis team? The international student association? . . . What else? Help me out.

STUDENT A: Pi Phi sorority.

STUDENT B: Exam study groups.

STUDENT C: Pre-med Club.

STUDENT D: Volunteers for Literacy.

STUDENT E: Film Club.

PROFESSOR: Good. Thanks. At any one time the average person belongs to five or six different groups. Our sense of identity comes largely from these groups. In fact, if I asked you to describe yourself, you would probably first tell me about what you do and what groups you belong to. You might say, "I'm a student, a member of the basketball team and the film club, and I'm a jogger," wouldn't you? Well, today we're going to look at two interesting aspects of group dynamics—that is, how groups function. We'll look first at patterns of communication in groups and then at how the group affects individual performance.

When we look at our own patterns of communication in groups, the communication seems unsystematic, random, unplanned, doesn't it? Generally, we don't see any pattern of communication at all. Think about the people in your discussion section yesterday. By the way, you all went to discussion section yesterday, didn't you? Well, did you notice the conversations before class?

STUDENT B: "Yeah. Everyone kept interrupting me."

PROFESSOR: Yes! And after class started, if you were having a good session, people kept interrupting each other and talking at the same time, didn't they? I'll bet students talked pretty much whenever they wished. At least that's what it seemed like. But researchers have looked closely at group dynamics and have found some very interesting patterns.

First of all, in groups where there is a lively discussion, everyone is not really talking at once. Actually, only a few people are talking. And it doesn't seem to matter how large the group is—only a few people talk at once. Do you know how many? Let's hear what you think . . .

STUDENT C: Three? A few is three, right?

STUDENT D: Well, maybe four?

STUDENT E: Could it be as few as two?

PROFESSOR: Yes, well, the answer is two. Two people do over 50 percent of the talking in any group.

Now whom do we talk to? When we're in a group situation, say, sitting around a table perhaps, whom do we tend to talk to? As an aside, I must comment here that all the research I know about has been done in the United States and Canada, so the results I have to share with you may only be valid in these countries. In other areas of the world it might be different. For example, the research findings I'm going to tell you about may not hold true for Mexico or Peru, Japan, Indonesia, Saudi Arabia, or even Germany.

Well, as I started to say, whom do people talk to when they're sitting together at a table—people across the table, or people sitting next to them?

MANY STUDENT VOICES: Across the table. Next to them.

PROFESSOR: Well, the research shows that in groups of eight or more, people tend to talk to the people sitting across the table from them, not to the people next to them. Here's an interesting possibility, if I may digress a bit. It seems to me that where I come from we have a social rule that doesn't make much sense, given what the research says about conversations at a table. The social rule is this: At a dinner party, a husband and wife are not supposed to be seated next to each other but are supposed to be seated across from each other instead. This is so they will have a chance to talk with the other guests—friends they don't see every day or people they have just met. However, the research suggests that they'll probably talk more with each other than with anyone else at the table. I suppose that would be nice if family life kept them so busy that they didn't have much time to talk at home. But still, the whole purpose of the social rule is defeated, don't you think? I think there are probably a lot of funny social rules like this—rules that don't make much sense anymore—but we'd better save that for another time.

Anyway, as I was saying, why do we tend to talk more to the people sitting opposite us? Probably because in our culture we usually want to have eye contact with the person we're talking to, and it's not as easy to have eye contact with someone who is sitting next to us. It's much easier to maintain eye contact with someone across the table.

To go somewhat off the topic again for a moment, if you're planning to be a matchmaker and start a romance between two of your friends, don't seat them next to each other at your next formal dinner party. On second thought, maybe seating them at a corner of the table would be best, wouldn't it? Then they would be very near each other and would only have to turn slightly in order to look into each others' eyes.

Well, back to business. Now there's one more point that I'd like to mention regarding conversation in groups, and this might be important to the new romance at your dinner party. Who knows? The research also shows that, in general, the person in the group who talks the most is regarded as the leader of the group. However, this person is not usually the most liked in the group, is he? D. J. Stang did some research that showed that the person in the group who talked a moderate amount was liked the most. What use can we make of this? A new romance would be affected by this aspect of group dynamics, wouldn't it?

But enough of romance and dinner parties. I now want to discuss another important aspect of group dynamics: the effect a group has on an individual's performance. If you look at the research, it turns out that sometimes the effect of the group on an individual's performance is positive, and sometimes it is negative. It took quite a while for social psychologists to figure out why this is true.

Some research showed that individuals did better on a task when they were doing it in a group. It didn't matter what the task was, slicing tomatoes or racing bicycles; individuals just performed better when other people were there. It also didn't matter whether the other people in the group were doing the task, too, or just watching, so competition was not a factor. The first person to notice this was Triplett.

STUDENT A: Excuse me, but what was his first name? It wasn't Tom, was it?

PROFESSOR: I'm sorry, it's slipped my mind, but I don't think it was Tom. Please come by my office if you want the complete reference. Anyway, Triplett's research was done quite a long time ago. In 1898, in fact. He watched bicycle racers and noticed that they did much better when there were other racers than when they raced only against the clock.

This behavior seemed unusual to him, so he conducted a simple experiment. He gave a group of children some fishing poles and string. The children were told to wind the string around the fishing poles as fast as possible. Half of the children worked alone. The others worked in pairs, groups of two. Interestingly, the children who worked in pairs worked faster than those who worked alone.

Well, you're probably not interested in winding string around fishing poles faster, but you are interested in doing math problems better, aren't you? F. H. Allport had people work on math problems alone and also in groups of five to six people. Individuals did better in the group situation than when they worked alone. The theory behind this type of research—research that demonstrates that people do better work in groups—is called "social facilitation theory."

Now here's an interesting aside. In this matter of having an audience, we're like a number of other creatures. We're like ants, for example. Chen did a laboratory experiment with ants. The ants were building nests. Chen arranged for some of the ants to work alone and for some of the ants to work with one or two other ants. Guess what! Ants worked harder—that is, they moved more balls of dirt—when they worked with other ants than when they worked alone. Similar results have been demonstrated with fish. But the most famous study was done with cockroaches. Zajonc—that rhymes with *science* but it's spelled z-a-j-o-n-c—Zajonc, Heingartner, and Herman watched cockroaches that were trying to get away from the light find their way through a maze. As you may know, cockroaches hate light. They are photophobic, right? The researchers arranged for the cockroaches to go through the maze without an audience of other cockroaches and also to do it with an audience of four other cockroaches. The cockroaches reached the end of the maze faster when they had an audience.

STUDENTS: No way! Really? You're kidding, right?

PROFESSOR: No, No! Really! This is true.

Well, to continue, as I mentioned earlier, there is also research that demonstrates that individuals perform worse, not better, on tasks when other people are there. The theory behind this research, research which shows that people do poorly in groups, is called "social inhibition theory." R. W. Hubbard did an interesting experiment. He had his subjects learn a finger maze. This is a maze that you trace with your finger. The subjects who had an audience did worse than the subjects who did the maze alone.

Now how can we explain these contradictory results? It seemed very confusing for a long time. Zajonc finally cleared up the confusion about why people sometimes perform better and sometimes worse in front of an audience. Zajonc found that the presence of an audience facilitates what you already know how to do. That is, if you know what you are doing, having an audience helps you do it better. If you are winding string around a fishing pole, you will do it better if there are other people there. But if you don't already know how to do something, you will probably make some mistakes. And you will make mistakes for a longer time if you have an audience. That's exactly what happened to the subjects who were learning the finger maze.

So if you are doing well, having an audience increases the chances that you will continue to do well. If you are doing badly, having an audience increases the chances that you will continue to do badly. Zajonc cleverly pointed out that when you are first learning something you are better off working alone than practicing with other people.

And let me mention that if you can manage it, you should take tests on a stage with a group of people who are also taking the test in front of a large audience. Not very practical though, is it? And I wonder if it's really true for every task we learn to do. What do you think? Well, let that be the first question for discussion next time. Thank you. See you then.

Asking for Information, Seeking Confirmation, and Challenging with Tag Questions

SKILL **B**

Conversations

Listen to the following conversations that include tag questions.

CONVERSATION 1

Steven is telling Tom about the first soccer practice of the season, which is only two days away. Listen to the speakers and answer the question.

STEVEN: Our team is having the first practice of the season this Saturday morning at eight. You'll be there, Tom, won't you?

TOM: Oh sure! I'll be there early.

Question: What intonation pattern does Steven use—genuine question, rhetorical question, or challenging question?

CONVERSATION 2

Steven and Tom have been looking forward to playing soccer on Saturday all week. Steven is telling a third friend, George, about the practice. Listen to the speakers and answer the question.

STEVEN: Our team is having the first practice of the season this Saturday morning at eight, George. You'll be there, Tom, won't you?

TOM: Sure will.

Question: What intonation pattern does Steven use this time—genuine question, rhetorical question, or challenging question?

CONVERSATION 3

Soccer practice has been arranged for 6:30 A.M. because another team has reserved the field for 8:30. Tom and Steven are talking about Karl, who told Tom that he wouldn't be coming until eight. Listen to the speakers and answer the question.

STEVEN: Soccer practice is at 6:30 A.M. this Saturday because another team has the field at 8:30.

TOM: Steve, Karl told me he can't come to soccer practice until eight.

STEVEN: What a drag. He's always late. He thinks he's coming at eight, does he? Well, I think he's off the team then. He can't come and go as he pleases and still be on the team.

Question: What intonation pattern does Steven use here—genuine question, rhetorical question, or challenging question?

CONVERSATION 4

Charlie's boss expects a report on Friday but realizes that it would be useful at a meeting on Wednesday. Listen to the speakers and answer the question.

BOSS: Charlie, I've got an unexpected merchandising meeting this week. The report won't be done by Wednesday, will it?

CHARLIE: Well, I don't think so, but we'll work on it.

Question: What intonation pattern does the boss use—genuine question, rhetorical question, or challenging question?

CONVERSATION 5

Josie comes home and sees Peter, one of her housemates, sitting in the living room with his feet up. Since it's already six o'clock, she concludes that it's not his turn to cook. Listen to the speakers and answer the question.

JOSIE: Hi, Pete. How are you?

PETE: Fine, how 'bout you?

JOSIE: Good. You're not cooking tonight, huh?

PETE: You got it. It's Barry's turn, right?

JOSIE: I think so, but he's going to be late again. I know it.

PETE: I think so too. Let's start the soup, okay? Otherwise, it'll be nine o'clock before we ever get anything to eat.

JOSIE: Okay, you're right and I'm starved. You cut the carrots and I'll do the potatoes.

Question: What single-word tag questions are used in this conversation?

Focus on Testing

You will hear two conversations. After each conversation, you will hear a question. To answer the question, read the four possible answers and decide which one is the best answer. Circle the letter of the best answer.

CONVERSATION 1

BILLY: This looks like the right size tennis racket, doesn't it? Try a few out. I'm going to look at the golf clubs.

ALEX: You'll come back and help me with this in a few minutes, won't you?

BILLY: Sure. Just as soon as I pick out a new driver.

Question: Where does this conversation take place?

CONVERSATION 2

MAN: Tom can get enough votes to win the election, can't he?

WOMAN: Well, if he gets the Asian, the African American, and the Native American special interest groups on his side, he can't lose, can he?

Question: What is the woman saying?

Crime and Punishment

LECTURE   *Choice: The Uniquely Human Problem*

PROFESSOR: I hope this thing is on. Yep. I guess it's on. Well, now that I've got your attention, we need to get started. I hope you remember our discussion of choice and free will. Last time we met, someone mentioned that it appears that we make choices all the time. Even not making a choice is a kind of choice, although it's obviously a rather passive one. In that case we are choosing not to choose. But as we also mentioned last time, the continuing philosophical dilemma that remains is: Do we ever really choose anything at all, or does it only appear that we do? Today I want to present a few more ideas on the notion of choice, a uniquely human problem.

What if our lives are totally predetermined? What if everything we do has already been decided for us before we are born? Maybe our genetic makeup programs us to do the things we do. Some people believe that some higher power makes all our decisions for us.

But even if we believe our lives are somehow predetermined, we still appear to be making choices every day. We decide what to have for dinner or what movie to go to. We choose our friends from among the hundreds of people we meet. Are these really choices, or is the concept of free choice only an illusion?

The opposite view is that we do, in fact, make all of our own decisions without any outside influence. For example, the Hindus and Buddhists believe that the sum of our freely made decisions add up to the kind of life we live. This is called karma. Further, they believe in reincarnation. According to this belief, if we don't make enough good decisions during one lifetime, we are given a chance to come back and try to do better in the next life.

These two opposing views, that everything is predetermined and that everything is self-chosen, can have important effects on our lives. Our attitudes and actions toward ourselves and others are often unconsciously determined by one or the other of these two views. Whether you are an optimist or a pessimist may have a lot to do with which view you hold. Why do you think this might be? I could use some of your thoughts on this. Yes, Craig.

CRAIG: Well, if you believe that everything has already been chosen for you . . . Well, then that might make you feel as if you have no control over what happens to you . . . you know . . . no control over any of the events in your life. I think this belief would definitely tend to make you pessimistic, rather than optimistic.

PROFESSOR: Yes, that's quite possible. Therefore, we need to examine these opposing views about choice as a starting point in determining our own attitude toward life. You may recall that Socrates suggested this when he said that the "unexamined life is not worth living."

Now let's consider some more mundane or practical aspects of choice. How many of you have looked at your past actions and said, "I wish I had done that differently"? Or "If only I had decided to do this instead of what I did." And certainly we all have worried about the future and sighed, "I hope I can do the right thing." Our relationship to the past and to the future seems to be intimately connected with our present choices. Not only are our present choices influenced by our past choices, but they influence our future choices as well. That is, all our "I wishes" and "I hopes" for the future are rooted in what we choose now, in the present.

Our awareness of the practical implications of choice intensifies when life-or-death decisions have to be made. For example, if you were a judge given the job of sentencing a person to prison or even death for violation of certain rules or beliefs of your community, you might deeply question the nature of "right" and "wrong" before finally deciding the case. Many of you may recall the harsh, inhuman condemnation of Jean Valjean described so powerfully by Victor Hugo in his novel *Les Misérables*. Jean Valjean was condemned to seven years of slavery for stealing a loaf of bread for his starving family. At the time the story took place, this was considered fair—a proper choice by the judge. Is this fair? What criteria of right and wrong apply here? What choice would you have made if you were the judge? I hope you would at least consider all the possible choices.

STUDENTS: Gee, that's a tough one. I don't know. I'm really not sure. I need to think about that one.

PROFESSOR: And what if you were Jean Valjean? Would you have chosen to break the law to feed your family?

STUDENTS: Absolutely! Of course! I'd have to! You bet your life I would!

PROFESSOR: OK. All right then. But now I want you to think about this. Would you then claim that you were not really responsible for the crime? Would you try to "get off" by claiming you did it because you were oppressed by the upper classes of society or because you and your family were so hungry? The hunger of your family? Hmm? You're not so quick to answer this time, are you?

Now, what about this case? On March 30, 1981, the president of the United States, Ronald Reagan, and three other men were shot on a street in Washington, D. C. John Hinckley, Jr., the young man who shot these men, admitted that he felt no remorse about his crime. Three of his four victims recovered; the fourth suffered permanent brain damage.

Fifteen months later, after an eight-week trial costing $3 million, Hinckley was found "not guilty by reason of insanity." Think about that. Hinckley shot the president of the United States and was merely sent to a mental hospital for counseling and treatment. When the psychiatrists decide that he is well enough, he will be released and sent home.

STUDENTS: Wow! That's incredible! No kidding! I didn't know that!

PROFESSOR: I assure you that it's true. Naturally, many people were outraged at such a light sentence and perhaps for good reason. However, that aspect of Hinckley's case is not my focus here. I want to focus instead on the choice Hinckley made. His actions stemmed from his choice, and his actions injured many people.

Did you know that in the United States we punish only those criminals whose choices have been made consciously, willfully, and freely? Yup, that's the law. If it can be shown in a court of law that an act, no matter how evil, was caused by influences beyond the control of the person who did it, that person is relieved of bearing the consequences of such an act.

In other words, in our society the law does not hold you responsible for choices you made when you were what is called "temporarily insane." What do think about that?

We are faced with other questions—perhaps not as serious—every moment of our lives. "Who will I go out with on Saturday night? And who will I marry? Shall I go on a diet? Should I go to the movies tonight or should I study for that biology test? Can I live just for today or had I better make long-range plans for my career? Should I tell the person who cut in line ahead of me at the supermarket that he's a jerk? How should I treat other people?

The poetry, fiction, and theater of every culture reflect the drama involved in making these kinds of choices, but they offer only tentative answers. The only definite rule we are given about making choices is that we have to make them or they will be made for us. Ah, but if only we could make perfect choices, then there would be no problem, right?

In summary, we have looked a little at crime and punishment and touched lightly on the extremely weighty and important matter of human choice. I hope this lecture has stimulated you to think about your own choices. All of us could use more time to reflect on our personal choices. For, after all, to choose is to be human.

SKILL **B**   *Expressing Wishes, Hopes, and Desires*

Conversations

Listen to the following conversation, which includes expressions of wishes, hopes, and desires. Write down all the expressions you hear. Compare notes with your classmates.

LAURA: Have you found a house to rent yet?

JAMES: No, not yet. I certainly hope I find one soon. My family is arriving in a few days, and I want to have a house ready for them when they get here.

LAURA: Sounds like you could use some help.

JAMES: Well, maybe a little, but probably all I really need is more money. If only I didn't have to find something inexpensive. I wish I were making a bit more money. Then I would have more choices of houses.

LAURA: Well, I may be able to help you out there.

JAMES: You mean you know of a good house for us?

LAURA: Not exactly. But I might know of a way for you to make some easy money making some quick deliveries.

JAMES: Uh-oh. This sounds too easy to be legal. But, I tell you, I'm getting really desperate at this point. I just might be tempted anyway.

LAURA: Well, I certainly hope you're just kidding. But this time you don't have to worry. It's definitely not illegal. I heard that Pizza Time wants someone to deliver pizzas from six to nine every night. And the pay's not bad.

JAMES: Oh, is that all? Well, that sounds great! Who do I talk to?

Focus on Testing

You will hear two conversations. After each conversation, you will hear a question. To answer the question, read the four possible answers and decide which one is the best answer. Circle the letter of the best answer.

CONVERSATION 1

ALLAN: My brother almost stole a car once.

EMILY: Allan, you're kidding! How did you stop him?

ALLAN: I asked him, "Do you want to go to jail?" And he said, "No." Then I told him, "If you can't do the time, don't do the crime."

EMILY: That's great. I bet the thought of time in jail changed his mind.

Question: What was Allan saying to his brother?

CONVERSATION 2

MARIA: Oh, Carla. I wish I were rich and famous.

CARLA: Are you sure that's what you want, Maria? There's an old saying: Be careful what you wish for because you might get it.

Question: What is Carla trying to tell Maria?

CHAPTER eleven

The Physical World

<u>LECTURE</u>   *Penguins at the Pole*

PROFESSOR GILL: Good Morning.

CLASS: Good Morning.

PROFESSOR GILL: Well, to continue with our study of polar ecosystems, I've arranged a special treat for you today. I've invited Professor Byrd, who has just returned from a two-year field study in the polar regions, to come and speak with us. He's going to share a few things about a part-time polar resident—the penguin—and its place in the polar ecosystem.

PROFESSOR BYRD: Hello. I see that you're all smiling. It never fails! Every time it's announced that my lecture will be about penguins, everyone immediately seems more gentle and cheerful. This is not surprising, seeing as how no one can resist these awkward little creatures that seem to be dressed in black and white suits. I don't know. Maybe we just identify with our own awkwardness when we have to wear formal suits.

Well, to begin. You know that the polar regions are like vast and desolate icy deserts and that only the hardiest forms of life survive there. It seems strange that this harsh land could be the spring and summer home of a migratory bird—the penguin.

Did I say bird? It also seems strange to call something that cannot fly a bird. But that's not all! The penguin is a tireless swimmer and is affectionate, considerate, and loyal—rare qualities in the bird kingdom. On account of this, this delightful creature is the "first citizen," so to speak, of the Antarctic.

The penguin is a key resident of this extremely spare ecosystem. In the Antarctic, all the activity of the ecosystem takes place on a thin shelf of land next to the great dome of ice that covers most of the region. It is to this bit of beachfront that the penguin comes to mate and raise its young. It's a little cold and slippery for volleyball at this beach, though.

Well, the Adélie penguin arrives with the relative warmth of spring, when the temperature rises above zero degrees Fahrenheit. That would be at about minus seventeen degrees Centigrade. Right away the penguin begins a long fast, a period in which it does not feed. During the previous months, the animals fed continuously on shrimp and small fish in warmer water, and they now have a store of fat to carry them through the months ahead. Owing to these fat reserves, they are able to swim hundreds of miles to the familiar ground of the bleak Antarctic shore.

When the penguins arrive at the nesting ground, their first task is to pair up—to mate—and to begin a kind of "civilized" life. Since as many as 50,000 birds may congregate at a time, there is definitely a need for order and tidiness. Because of this need, penguins build nests in such perfect rows that the nesting area resembles the streets of a city.

However, this order is often interrupted by battles between birds. These small wars may be fought by two male birds over a particularly adorable female or by a male and a female as they settle the marriage contract. These little battles go on constantly for several weeks, until the pairs, or mates, are settled. The penguins never actually kill one another, but it is not unusual to see bloodstains and broken wings. The winners of these love battles have won a relationship with a female that is the most extraordinary in the animal world. There seems to be a blissful understanding between the mates. I've observed the delicate and gracious way they treat each other, at times standing very close and swaying back and forth as if to celebrate their union. The losers, the males that fail to find a suitable mate, move to the edge of the nesting ground. These birds become the "hooligans," or delinquents, of the group. They steal unguarded eggs, disturb nests, and play jokes on the happy couples.

STUDENT A: I think we have a few of those hooligan types here in town.

PROFESSOR BYRD: Yes, I've seen that behavior myself. So. . . . After nearly a month of fasting, the eggs are laid in little nests made of stones by the males. Then family life begins. Although the brooding instinct is very strong and parental care is truly dedicated, as many as 75 percent of the eggs are lost due to catastrophic floods caused by melting ice, the death of the parents, burial of the nests by landslides or heavy snows, the vandalism of the "hooligan" males I mentioned before, and, of course, the eating of the eggs by other birds.

CLASS: Gee! That's awful! That's so sad! Oh, no!

PROFESSOR BYRD: Yes, it's sad, but some eggs do survive, of course, and once the chicks begin to hatch, the penguin colony teems with life. The long fast is over, and the parents take turns feeding and bringing back food for the new penguin chick.

It is during this period that the comical character of the penguin is revealed. They often feed in large groups, walking or sliding for miles in single-file lines to the ocean. There they dare one another to jump into the water. They often approach the edge of a cliff and then retreat several times.

Once one brave penguin dives in, however, the others follow almost at once, leaping from exactly the same spot. In the water, they engage in various water sports that they've invented while they gorge themselves on shrimp and other small sea creatures.

It's not all fun and games, however. Even though their black and white markings help to hide them, there is little the penguins can do to protect themselves from the jaws of the sea leopard. This fearsome creature looks like a cross between a seal and a great white shark. Some of you might remember the movie *Jaws*?

CLASS: Yeah! Sure! Right!

STUDENT A: Sure we do! Duh-Da-Duh-Da-Da Da Da

PROFESSOR BYRD: Well, the sea leopard jaw is just as mean! The sea leopard is a very big seal with many large, sharp teeth, a nasty disposition, and a fondness for penguin meat. Even though penguins are excellent swimmers, it is difficult for them to escape these ferocious attackers.

For this reason, the group is smaller in number when it returns to the nesting ground. But penguins are generous creatures and food is shared with the orphaned chicks—those whose parents have not returned. Adult penguins also share babysitting duties. One bird will watch over a number of chicks while the others play.

STUDENT B: Even the males?

PROFESSOR BYRD: Especially the males!

STUDENT B: Hear that, Frank?

PROFESSOR BYRD: Oh, Yes. They share everything. And they love to visit with neighbors, explore nearby ice floes, and even climb mountains, following the leader in long lines up the mountainside.

When the domesticity of the mating season finally comes to an end, the penguins line up in ranks like little black and white soldiers and prepare to march to the sea. At some signal that is imperceptible to humans, they suddenly begin their orderly walk. At the edge of the sea, they stand as if at attention again, waiting for a signal. When it is given, they begin their swim to their winter home on another part of the continent.

Well, I think I'm keeping you a bit late. If Professor Gill will invite me back maybe we can continue talking about penguins another time.

CLASS: Yes! That's would be great! Please come back!

PROFESSOR GILL: Definitely. I think that can be arranged. Thank you so much, Professor Byrd. We've enjoyed your talk immensely.

SKILL B — *Stating Reasons*

Conversations

Listen to the following conversation which contains several different ways of stating reasons. List all of the expressions used to state reasons on the following lines. Compare your list with your classmates' lists.

SARAH: Hello?

JOHN: Hello. Sarah? This is John.

SARAH: John! Hello! How nice to hear from you. I thought you'd left to do your field study already.

JOHN: No, not yet. We ran into a few problems. Some of our specialized equipment hasn't arrived yet. On account of this we may have to put off the field trip until next year.

SARAH: I'm sorry to hear that, but couldn't you leave as soon as the equipment arrives?

JOHN: Well, ordinarily we might, but in view of the fact that the field trip was to be in Antarctica, there's yet another problem.

SARAH: Really? What's that?

JOHN: Well, it's almost winter there now, and since our study will take several months, we'll have to wait at least until next spring. It's just too cold to do much outdoor study there in the winter.

SARAH: Well, it's too bad about having to cancel your field trip, but since you're still in town, why don't you come over for a visit tonight?

JOHN: I was hoping you'd say that! I'd love to.

Focus on Testing

You will hear two conversations. After each conversation, you will hear a question. To answer the question, read the four possible answers and decide which one is the best answer. Circle the letter of the best answer.

CONVERSATION 1

COLLEGE DEAN: Since you won't be joining the Antarctica expedition this year, would you reconsider our offer to join the staff here at Elmhurst?

EXPLORER: Thank you again for the offer, Dean Hemmings, but the reason I refused still holds. I just don't think I'm cut out for teaching.

Question: What is the man refusing?

CONVERSATION 2

MAN: In view of the fact that people are ignoring the importance of the ecology of the polar regions, I think we're headed for catastrophe.

WOMAN: Oh, you mean like a worldwide drought caused by global warming or severe flooding in coastal cities?

Question: What is the man implying?

CHAPTER twelve

Together on a Small Planet

LECTURE   *Folk Wisdom*

PROFESSOR: Let's see. Today we're going to be talking about folk wisdom.

Most people like to give advice. Occasionally, people give advice in a particularly memorable way, and we end up repeating their advice—often in the form of quotations or sayings—to our friends and family members. This type of advice is special because it provides insight into those things that are most universal in life—marriage, death, friendship, money, religion, and love—to name a few.

Every culture has a wealth of sayings that serve to guide behavior. These sayings are part of what is commonly referred to as "folk wisdom." Of course, folk wisdom can also be expressed in other ways, such as myths, fairy tales, legends, and songs. Often, however, folk wisdom is shared in the form of short, often humorous sayings about the best ways to approach life's joys and sorrows.

Today, we'll look at some of the humorous sayings of three famous Americans: Benjamin Franklin, Abraham Lincoln, and Mark Twain. Then I'll ask you to share some examples of folk wisdom from your own cultures.

One characteristic of American folk wisdom is its blend of wisdom and humor. Humor makes the bitter medicine of life easier to swallow. It takes the harsh realities of life and places them in colorful wrappers, making them more attractive. For example, Ben Franklin's clever saying, "A full belly makes a dull brain" could also be rendered, "People who are well-fed or self-satisfied can become lazy and stupid." However, the second version has none of the elegance and humor of the first. Most moralists in the United States are successful because they are able to say wise things humorously.

Ben Franklin was the first of America's respected humorists. Franklin himself led a lusty and robust life. He liked to eat, drink, and be merry, but he never tired of telling others to practice chastity and moderation—for example, this famous quotation: "Early to bed and early to rise makes a man healthy, wealthy, and wise." This contrast between Franklin's words and behavior illustrates the first rule of moralizing: You don't have to live a good life to "talk" one.

But for Franklin this was all part of the joke, and he lived to a ripe old age to laugh about it. His *Poor Richard's Almanac* is filled with good ideas on how to live a happy life. For example, he advised, "Keep your eyes wide open before marriage and half-shut afterwards." And, "Three may keep a secret if two of them are dead." His comment about the postal system holds true today: "If you want a thing done, go—if not, send." And, of course, this comment speaks about action in general. That is, if you want to be sure something gets done, do it yourself. In spite of his support for the American revolution, he once wrote: "There never was a good war or a bad peace." "God heals and the doctor takes the fees," and "Nothing is more fatal to health than overcare of it." Franklin's style was sensible, easy, simple, colloquial, and homespun.

Abraham Lincoln, although less poetic than Franklin, expressed similar opinions about life. Lincoln continued the tradition of "horse sense" humor that was begun by Davy Crockett, who was called "the coonskin philosopher" because of the raccoon-skin cap he always wore. "Horse sense" is truth expressed in simple terms. "Make sure you're right, then go ahead" is a quote from Crockett. This type of humor appeals to people who hunger for practical common sense.

Lincoln understood people's need for "horse sense." Both a politician and an idealist, he knew how to use common sense to serve his own ends. He could take the highest moral principles or the most critical observations and dress them in a folksy humor that would make them better understood and more easily accepted by everyone. For example, this quote, which is one of best known in the United States: "You can fool all of the people some of the time, and some of the people all of the time, but you can't fool all of the people all of the time." Another of Lincoln's wise and seemingly unsophisticated statements is: "The Lord prefers common-looking people. That is why he makes so many of them."

There is no doubt that people need a little push sometimes to help them see the folly of their ways. Mark Twain used humor to reveal that many cherished ideas were false, foolish, or even harmful. Twain seemed to think that most human beings were ignorant of the forces controlling their lives and were too easily manipulated by those in authority. He felt that it was easier for people to be "misled" than to be led correctly, so he used all his skill to expose the stupidity of those in power. For example, he said, "Hain't we got all the fools in town on our side and ain't that a big enough majority in any town?"

People in power often use statistics to further an argument, and Twain had a comment to make about this too. He said, "There are three kinds of lies—lies, damned lies, and statistics." Like Franklin and Lincoln, he also gave good advice. He said, for example, "It is by the goodness of God that we have in our country three unspeakably precious things: freedom of speech, freedom of conscience, and the prudence never to practice either." This is quite a strong statement on how to get along with other people.

After reading a small sample of Twain, you might get the impression that he was a misanthrope, a person who found fault with everyone. It's true that his humor was sometimes harsh, but it was used to cut away all the pretensions and vanities of human relationships. The result, Twain thought, would be a more just society. Twain was fully aware that he irritated a lot of people. One of his most famous comments came in a telegram he sent from Europe to the Associated Press. It read, "The reports of my death are greatly exaggerated."

Well, now. The students in this class come from a lot of different backgrounds. How about sharing with the group some of the sayings, some of the folk wisdom, from your culture? Dimitri, what about starting with you? Can you give us a saying from Greece?

DIMITRI: Well . . . Here's one: "The beginning is half of every action."
PROFESSOR: That's certainly true. Just getting started is often the hardest part. Vijay, do you know any Hindu sayings?
VIJAY: Oh, yes: "It's no sin to kill the killer." But, actually, I don't agree with this saying.
PROFESSOR: That's definitely a discussion we should take up some time. Brigitta, what about the Dutch?
BRIGITTA: I really like this one: We say, "Nobody's sweetheart is ugly."
PROFESSOR: Dan. Can you tell us a Native American saying that you really like?

DAN: You probably know this one: "Don't judge a man until you have walked two moons in his moccasins."

BRIGITTA: Dan, what are moccasins?

DAN: They're a kind of shoe.

BRIGITTA: Oh, now I see.

PROFESSOR: Yes, I have heard that one, Dan. Thank you. Mohammed, what about you?

MOHAMMED: If a camel once gets his nose in the tent, his body will follow.

PROFESSOR: That's great! I had never heard that one. Tetsuzo, do you have a favorite folk saying from your country?

TETSUZO: Yes, I do. "To kick with a sore toe only hurts the foot."

PROFESSOR: I had never heard that one either. It makes a lot of sense. And who's left? Ahmet. How about a Turkish saying?

AHMET: Well, we love coffee, you know. So we say: "Coffee should be as black as hell, as strong as death, and as sweet as love."

PROFESSOR: Oh, yes. Very good. Well, that's all we have time for. Now as you work on your presentations, remember what Mark Twain said, "It takes more than three weeks to prepare a good impromptu speech."

SKILL B — *Telling a Joke*

Conversations

You will hear a group of students who are taking a break, sitting in the student union, hanging out, and telling jokes. As you listen, notice how the students introduce the four jokes they tell. Then answer the questions.

JIMMY: Hi, guys. What's up?

FRANK: Oh, nothing. We're just sitting around having coffee, telling jokes.

CATHERINE: Yeah, like the one my teacher told in education class. Once there was a teacher who was telling about how machines help people and she asked a student, "John, can you name a great timesaver?" "Yes," John replied. "Love at first sight."

JIMMY: Oh, Catherine, that's sweet. I've spent a lot of time in New York, and I love to tell the one about the boy who asked for directions to a famous concert hall. "Sir," he asked an old gentleman, "How do you get to Carnegie Hall?" The old man replied, "Practice, my son, practice."

JIMMY: You groaned the loudest, Joanna, so you go next.

JOANNA: Have you heard the one about the man who was dining in an expensive restaurant and the waiter came by and asked, "How did you find your steak, sir?" and the man answered, "Purely by accident. I moved the potatoes and the peas, and there it was."

FRANK: I like the one about the little girl who was asked, "Sally, when you get as big as your mother, what will you do?" and Sally answered quite seriously, "Diet."

JIMMY: Hey, you guys. Enough of this. I've got to go study.

CATHERINE: Me too. See you guys later.

ALL: Bye. See you later. Have a good one.

Question 1: Catherine tells a joke that she heard her teacher tell. How does Catherine introduce the joke?

Question 2: Jimmy tells a joke about a boy in New York City. How does Jimmy introduce his joke?

Question 3: Joanna tells a joke about a man in a restaurant. How does Joanna introduce her
joke?

Question 4: Frank tells a joke about a little girl. How does Frank introduce the joke?

Focus on Testing

You will hear two conversations. After each conversation, you will hear a question. To answer
the question, read the four possible answers and decide which one is the best answer. Circle the
letter of the best answer.

CONVERSATION 1

NORMAN: Julie, have you heard the one about the two penguins having a drink at a bar?

JULIE: Oh, no, Norman. Not another weird joke.

NORMAN: O.K., how about the one about the chicken and the duck?

JULIE: No, no. Gimme a break.

Question: Why is Julie refusing to listen to Norman?

CONVERSATION 2

HAROLD: I'm not sure whether I should tell that story about Mr. Leonard at the Awards Dinner.
What do you think?

SUSAN: Well, you're a good storyteller, but I'm not sure people would find it all that
interesting.

HAROLD: What are you trying to say, Susan?

SUSAN: In a word—when in doubt, leave it out.

Question: What does Susan mean?